seeking safety

"A sequel to the young adult drama novel Needing Normal, Emme Grange's Seeking Safety continues the story of Jett Harper and her friends as the sophomore year comes with its own set of challenges... Seeking Safety delves into some heavy topics, such as teenage anxiety, poverty, and racism. Author Emme Grange delivers a considerate and authentic portrayal of a teenager on the autistic spectrum coming to terms with her first brush with real-world issues when it impacts those closest to her. The narrative flows past without a single hitch as Grange handles some sensitive subject matter with the required nuance and subtlety that it deserves. The characters are grounded and relatable. Jett is an immensely sympathetic protagonist you find yourself caring for from the very first page. Her relationships with the rest of the members of the Core5 continue to develop and grow stronger by the day. A relevant book I highly recommend to teenagers and young adults."

Pikasho Deka for *Readers' Favorite*

"Seeking Safety tells a realistically complex story from the perspective of a neuro-diverse character, which is what I loved most about this world that Emme Grange has created... Sensitive topics such as disabilities, poverty, racism, and police brutality are addressed and challenged in such ways that readers can easily empathize with Jett and her experiences. With shocking moments and the overall suspense of trying to discover what happened to Sam, it seems that Jett's life never has a dull moment, and the book is impossible to put down. I look forward to reading more about Jett and what awaits her and her friends during their adventures in high school."

Amy Powers for *Readers' Favorite*

Seeking Safety by Emme Grange brings us the story of the Core5 members during their sophomore year at Presidio Prep in San Francisco... At fifteen, sifting through all the different emotions and getting ready for real life can be extremely challenging for anyone. For Jett, things aren't always so simple...

The intensity of emotion saturates Seeking Safety on every page. Where else can it go but be absorbed by the reader? Emme Grange has done a magnificent job at helping the reader have a small shred of understanding of what it is to be normal and atypical. The characters are vibrant, full, and relatable. I love the fact that consideration is the main character's superpower! I also found solace in the character of Joe Harper and how he explained things. Important tools for grounding will help both typical and atypical individuals. The importance of family and friends and the support they offer is key in this story. Determination and perseverance also play a huge role. I will admit that a book that has me smiling and crying all at once is one of a kind! While this book is more geared toward younger adults, I believe everyone will benefit from having met Jett.

Ronél Steyn for *Readers' Favorite*

"Emme Grange has an easy-flowing writing style which she uses successfully in Seeking Safety to address some of the social issues affecting today's youth. She cleverly portrays the oblivious state in which many upper-class individuals live, unaware of the significant effects of poverty and discrimination against individuals based on their race. In all this, the team, Core5, develops an even stronger bond with each other while addressing the state of safety in their school. Grange shows that friendship can blossom between people unexpectedly and that an emotional bond is stronger than your social class."

Delene Vrey for *Readers' Favorite*

★ ★ ★ ★ ★

"Emme Grange's characters are real and their experiences portray a world that most readers have known. I enjoyed the intelligently crafted banter, the strong conflict, and the crisp prose... Seeking Safety: Sophomore Year is a novel for readers who love being transported back to high school days and who enjoy good storytelling craft."

Divine Zape for *Readers' Favorite*

Seeking Safety
Sophomore Year

Copyright © 2022
by aTYPICAL AUTHOR press for Emme Grange.

All rights reserved.

aTYPICAL AUTHOR press supports the integrity of intellectual property and the value of copyright. The purpose of copyright is to encourage individuals to produce the creative works that enrich our culture.

ANY distribution of an authors' intellectual property without their express written permission, other than limited excerpts for review purposes, is considered theft and expressly prohibited.

If you would like to obtain permission to use material from this book or any other works by Emme Grange, please contact her directly emme@emmegrange.com. Thank you for your support of the author's rights.

Cover design by Cover Culture
Interior formatting by Alt 19 Creative

ISBN 978-1-955856-05-8 (pb) / 978-1-955856-06-5 (e)

Published by:

aTYPICAL
AUTHOR
press

*This one is dedicated to all those who are seeking safety.
I believe safety is a foundational building block
for a better life, for a better world.
We can create that, together.*

seeking safety

LIFE AS JETT HARPER was only getting better. Better than she had ever thought possible. A week ago, Sam sent Jett a text inviting her to the Orpheum Theater to see "Hamilton." It had taken Jett a moment to reply, simply because she knew how expensive the tickets must have been, and she didn't know how to respond without bringing that up. She wanted to figure out how to say yes to such a fabulous night out, but not without contributing. That wouldn't be right. Over the last school year, Sam had revealed she was poor, not in those words exactly, but in many other ways. So how had she come by tickets? Jett didn't need to wait long for an answer. A new text from Sam arrived.

> My sister, Miya, got us really good seats. She's in the show now. So... what do you say? Want to meet me there?

Jett's stomach somersaulted as she gripped her phone. She couldn't respond fast enough.

> Yes, please!!!

As the invitation settled in, her pulse started to race. *Finally*, she would experience the show everyone constantly inserted into everyday conversations for herself! Plus, she had done her research on best friends. Anxious to know whether Sam also wanted to be "besties," she had been preparing. Even though lots of data points written on sticky notes fought for space on her whiteboard about "Being a Bestie," Jett was most excited that Sam had invited her to go to "Hamilton." It meant they were *probably* on the same page, labels-wise. Last year at this time, with the end of summer closing in before her freshman year of high school, Jett hadn't had a single friend her age. In fact, she'd never had a friend her age. Ever. Now she had 3.5 friends and one of those could soon claim the specific role of Best Friend.

To ensure she did things right, Jett asked Mother for help. When she had asked to be taken shopping for a special outfit for her night out, Mother had been so happy that Jett believed she may have even cried a little. At least, she beamed with pleasure and her eyes looked glassy. Jett remembered back to last year's winning project for the Freshman Faire. Quality time was her Mother's top love

Seeking Safety

language and yet, to Jett, spending time the way Mother liked to meant that Jett would have an opportunity to hone her acts of service. She made a note on her phone to remember to do that for Mother again, even if it meant sitting through inane chatter about nothing important while they got their nails done. Again. She rolled her eyes. Totally acts of service from her point of view, although for her mom, it was quality time. People were so complicated!

Jett's breath mingled with crisp night air as she exhaled. Hands raised as she studied her nails, it looked like she was blowing on the sparkly black polish, but she wasn't. It was just that cold out. Waiting outside the theater after the show, she studied its iconic sign and savored the fact that she finally understood the fuss. She agreed with the general consensus; "Hamilton" had been amazing!

Sam and Jett stood close together by the Orpheum Theatre's stage door like all the other groupies and fans who wanted to meet cast and crew. Although Sam wasn't in a very talkative mood, Jett was. She wanted to know more about the sister Sam loved so much. "Tell me more about your Miya," she urged. "Does she love performing as much as it looks like it? I know she was not a main character, but she was so great!"

Head bowed, Sam's shoulders rose. She had been so silent and withdrawn all night that Jett was struggling to understand the cues. Why would Sam invite her and then remain silent?

Sam looked morose, and Jett wondered what she was supposed to do. Despite all her research on friendship, she had yet to find a manual that explained how to act when someone was acting out of character. Maybe she was doing this whole friendship thing wrong.

"My sister is the coolest sister in the whole world," Sam replied, tears welling in her eyes. "I don't know what else to say. It's been her and me for as long as I can remember, even before Grams took us in. Miya has always looked out for me and—"

Abruptly, Sam was interrupted when a scarred and battered door banged open. The air crackled with electrified excitement as everyone turned expectantly.

Jett watched actors coming outside search the crowd for familiar faces. Some found fans, some spotted friends, and others found family. A few of the cast and crew remained engaged in deep conversation with their peers. Jett peeked at Sam to see whether she might continue her revelation. No, it seemed like that might be on pause. That's okay. She could wait. It's what best friends did. Jett smiled to herself. With little conscious effort, she was already being a best friend.

Sam surveyed the passing cast members and swung into action when her eyes met her sister's. Miya waved off her friends and turned to Sam and Jett just as someone shouted to her. "Miya, are you sure you don't want to go to the cast party with us? Share a car? It sounds epic, and I'm sure you can bring those two."

"Nah! They're not old enough for that!" Miya replied. "We're going to head out. Maybe I'll meet up with you guys later!"

Two steps more and she was in front of them. "Hi there! You must be Jett and you both must be freezing. And I'm starving!" she said, beaming a smile at them. "Sam told me you want to treat us to Max's Opera Cafe! That's cool. I'm pretty sure they're still open." She draped an arm around Sam's shoulders and they started walking towards Opera Plaza.

Soon after entering Max's, they were tucked into a cozy booth awaiting a feast of sliders, fries, cheesecake, and a giant eclair. Jett could sense nebulous, somber undercurrents from both sisters, but didn't understand the cause. The show had been precise, fluid, complex, and enthralling. It was, in short, amazing. The wait to meet up with Miya had been cold, but bearable. Now, although there were three people in the booth, it didn't feel like it. Instead, it felt like Sam and Miya were speaking privately, without words, leaving Jett as a bystander. What was wrong? Did Miya need praise? Was her love language words of affirmation? It wouldn't hurt to tell her how well she performed, in any event. Right? She opened her mouth and was just about to speak when Miya caught her eye and shook her head no. Food began filling their table.

Jett took Miya's cue to heart and remained silent. She waited for someone to tell her what was going on. Was their grandmother all right? Obviously Miya was okay. What could be the matter? She looked up from a bite of the shared eclair and watched a tear slide down Sam's cheek. Jett watched as Miya smoothed Sam's hair.

And that was all it took for the floodgates to open. Suddenly, Sam was in her sister's arms, sobbing. Miya was doing her best to soothe Sam, but Jett felt helpless. The server came by, but Miya waved him off. She started crooning softly. Jett couldn't tell the song, but she saw its effect as Sam started to relax, her eyelids fluttering closed.

"It's all right, Boo," Miya murmured. "You rest some now, yeah? Use my lap as a pillow. This has all been too much for you." Jett watched as she ran her fingers along Sam's face like mothers with toddlers often did. This made sense to Jett; mothers probably taught big sisters how to comfort younger siblings. Was it something she was missing by not having a big sister? She tucked away that tidbit to examine later. Miya looked at Jett and nodded.

Nodded? Why? What did that mean? Did Miya read her thought process, and was she answering her question? Jett knew better than to speak yet, but she was so confused. What was too much? She watched the tenderness that infused every bit of how Miya treated Sam, and she wanted it. Jett wished she had a sister. If she had one, would her sister be able to explain to her what was going on? Or would her sister give her grief for her ignorance about something everyone else seemed to grasp easily? Jett heard Miya take in a breath as her soft song faded away.

"So, 'Jett,' huh? Like the retro rocker chick or like the color? Do you know where your name came from?" Miya peered into Jett's eyes, looking for something.

Jett lowered her gaze. She felt the intensity and deflated a bit when she realized she didn't know the origin of her name. Why didn't she know this already? She'd have to ask her parents.

"I don't know why my parents chose this name, to be honest," she said apologetically. "More importantly, though, can you tell me what's upsetting my friend? I've been trying to figure it out, but Sam doesn't talk about personal stuff a whole lot."

Miya nodded, gazing down at Sam for a moment before returning her attention to Jett.

"Yeah. I can tell you, but first I want to let you know that Sam probably tells you more than anyone else besides me," she said. "Did you know that? She's been telling me all about this cool kid named Jett in her classes ever since she started at that crazy school, Presidio Prep. Do you like it there?"

The change of subject startled Jett, but she replied confidently.

"I do. It's not at all what I expected, but that probably makes it better. There's a lot to adjust to, though. It's very different, very—" She paused, trying to think of the right words. "The setting is idyllic. Inspiring even. And I like that there are students from all over the Bay Area. They're diverse and yet they're not because everyone is so, *so* smart. It's the first time I'm not leagues ahead of all the other students." She paused to consider. "Did that sound rude? I don't mean to be rude."

Then Jett smiled as she and Miya said, in unison, "but facts are facts."

Miya laughed softly and looked back down at her sister.

"I'm pretty sure it's like that for Sam, too. She's used to being the smartest one in our 'hood. Suddenly she's telling me 'everyone is so smart.' And, for the first time ever, she wasn't going to have to do all the work on a group project."

She turned serious again. "Hey, detour: Tell me about what it's like to live with two parents and to be an only child. Do you have a lot of them in your neighborhood? Do your parents throw dinner parties and stuff?"

Jett laughed ruefully. "Um—no. I mean yes. I will tell you, but no—that is not my life. My dad is a lawyer and my mom is a therapist. They both work in San Francisco, so they both commute. Usually, they drive in together. Sometimes Mother takes the ferry in. We don't have kids in our neighborhood. It's full of old people." When she saw Miya smile at that, she backed up. "I mean adults. And they *do* socialize out and about. I'm expected to go along, for the most part, or they don't go. It's my dad's rule. If I can't go, he doesn't go."

Shrugging, she considered what else to add. "I only know what it's like to live with my two parents, so I can't really compare it to anything else. They're a funny pair, but they usually work together well and I learn a lot from them."

Jett took a deep breath, hoping she'd answered enough that Miya would now tell her what was going on with Sam.

"Please tell me what's wrong with Sam," she urged.

A slow, sad smile dimmed the glowing light of curiosity in Miya's eyes. It seemed like Miya was struggling to open up.

"I'm sorry little sis didn't tell you," said Miya, gently caressing Sam's hair. "This is our last performance in The City. We're moving on tomorrow to Los Angeles."

Jett was baffled. Was Sam leaving, too? Who exactly made up this 'we'? Involuntarily, Jett started wringing her napkin under the table. She looked at Miya expectantly and was glad when she continued.

"With me gone, Grams and Sam will have more space. And that's totally a good thing," Miya said, obviously trying to make the best of the situation. "Making a set amount of money each week while travelling and being part of this show is epic! I've been dreaming of this for so long, I sometimes have to pinch myself to know I'm awake and living it! I feel really good about it—" and here she paused, her voice catching "—until I think about leaving Sam. Of course, I'm gonna miss her like crazy, but I've got my show. I'm not the one left behind. I get to go on an adventure, to travel and perform. I mean, I've always wanted to be part of a touring cast. Not necessarily as a part of the chorus, but there is also something special about that. We get to have an instant group of friends, of people we are tied to, all for the same cause."

She had been stroking Sam's head as she spoke and paused again to gaze at her sister. She looked up. "I imagine that's kind of like you guys on your team project, right?" Jett nodded as Miya went on. "The Core 5, as Sam calls it. She really likes you and Andy and Carlos. She says Ruby Stefano is pretty much like you would expect her to be. Do you think that's true?"

Jett considered how to respond to this before answering. "Well, to be honest, I didn't know what to expect from Ruby. Or any of them, really. She is definitely the most famous of our group and I think she has a hard time adjusting to not having the support she's used to."

Jett paused and studied Sam's sleeping face. "I guess letting go of what we're used to can throw anyone for a loop, right? It makes me think about what you just told me about you and Sam. I imagine it's going to be a huge adjustment for her, too. Is there anything I can do?"

Really wanting to know, Jett waited. She needed insight. She needed direction. She hoped Miya would be specific and give her tasks so that Sam wouldn't stay so closed, so silent, so sad.

Miya studied her for a long moment before a big smile broke across her face. "Sam told me you like to take time to let information settle in while you figure things out and then your ideas are nothing short of super-cool. What I see, though, is that you honestly care about people. I mean really, really. Am I right?" Miya already was nodding to herself even before Jett nodded in agreement. She was still confused, though. Wasn't everyone like that?

"I think I'm right," Miya emphasized. "You're a good egg, Jett, a good, good egg."

Wait, Jett thought, looking away as she puzzled this through. How could a person be a good egg? Were some people bad eggs? But how was that even quantified? Good or bad egg people? She turned back to Miya, who seemed to be watching her absorb the information.

"Jett, I need you to do something for me, okay?"

Jett nodded, relieved to know that Miya would help her understand what to do for Sam.

"I need you to look out for my little sis. Sam may seem tough, but in a way, she's my baby! And I need her to be okay when I'm gone. Can you be here for her? Can you be her friend no matter what? Don't give up when she closes in on herself, okay? She's gonna need you. My Grams has her crew. They'll watch out for her, but Sam will be all alone and I'm worried about that. Will you be her one true friend?"

Jett kept nodding as she let this sink in. Of *course* she could be Sam's friend no matter what. This seemed an awful lot like being a best friend. Jett smiled broadly as she put that together. She was being asked to be Sam's best friend! It was the role she had researched and been preparing for since the end of the last school year. *Yes*! She could do that! A thousand times, yes!

"Of course I can be her one true friend while you're gone, and even when you're back. One true friend is like a best friend, right? Because Sam is already my best friend and I would like to be hers."

Miya reached over and squeezed Jett's hand for just a moment. "You're pretty cool, Jett. I'm glad Sam's your best friend and, yes, I am asking you to be hers. I'm warning you now. It won't always be easy. When she's moody, she's sarcastic. When she's upset, she gets too quiet. And when she feels anything or everything, she *needs* music."

She looked at Jett with imploring eyes. "Help her keep her music alive? Help her channel her feels?"

It seemed to Jett like Miya was making sure she understood, but all Jett could do was nod at her. She wanted to explain that she knew what it was like to feel so much you could scarcely breathe. She knew what it was like to have emotions and extra energy trapped in your body. She knew what it's like not to know what to do with it all. Could she be there for Sam? Jett locked onto Miya's eyes to emphasize her point.

"It would be my honor and my pleasure. Thank you for asking me. I am in Sam's corner. I won't give up. No matter what."

Satisfied, Miya gazed back down at her sister. "Okay Jett. I'm counting on you."

Jett followed her gaze and saw that Sam was stirring, finally, right on cue. It was time to go. The server had brought the check.

Outside, Sam and Miya waited for Jett's ride home.

"Miya, thank you for getting us tickets so we could witness your amazing performance. 'Hamilton' was amazing, life-changing, inspiring! And I'm glad you're a part of it." Jett was thinking about how awesome it was for Miya to follow her dreams—until she looked into Sam's sad face. Listless and lethargic, Sam looked weighed down with dread.

Watching out the car window for as long as she could see, Jett saw the two sisters clinging to each other. She memorized some of their final moments together and felt tears running down her own face. They fell onto her hand before she even knew that she, too, was crying. Jett vowed that nothing would stop her from being Sam's Best Friend.

2

BEING SUMMONED TO the family office meant serious business.

Jett knew it, experience proved it, and Daddio looked so somber. Just... why was she in trouble? She couldn't think of a reason, but that didn't stop her from worrying. Jett rocked back and forth on the balls of her feet as she waited for his attention.

Pacing the entire expanse of the room, Daddio kept speaking in low tones.

Was there someone else there? Maybe he was on the phone. Where was Mother? She sighed in relief, realizing it would be just the two of them today. As her rocking slowed, she noticed the moment Daddio spotted her.

He pasted on a smile and beckoned her into the office. It was time.

"Hey, Bug-a-boo. Tell me what's new?" Daddio's eyebrows shot up, as if he hadn't meant to rhyme and just now heard how his words had landed.

Jett thought this was pretty funny. So this wasn't a serious summons after all. She must have misinterpreted the whole thing. Shoulders falling in relief, she smiled back.

"As you know, I saw 'Hamilton' with my friend Sam last night. I think she's my best friend now. And thank you for buying us dinner. Max's was cool, but the show was incredible! I can't believe how fast they spoke—sang—whatever, up there on stage in front of everyone! Have you seen it in person? I can't remember. If you have, did you notice how precise, how intentional, every single movement was?"

Jett stopped for a beat and scratched at her temple, marveling. "I swear they knew who was exactly where and exactly what was happening at all times. I can't imagine what having that much awareness would be like, being able to track like that."

She hopped unconsciously from one foot to the other as she processed the evening's sensations. "Do you do that? Do you know where everyone is and what they're doing, all at the same time? I certainly don't. It would exhaust me, but watching it happen was stunning. Simply stunning. Like a ballet."

Realizing that she had been monologuing, Jett stopped abruptly. Again. "Is that what you wanted to know, or do you have something else in mind? I'm only wondering because you're wearing your discovery face."

This was a new term Jett recently adopted from her time with Darren, Daddio's partner in the law firm. He had pointed it out to her, and she memorized the label because it was a perfect description of what she had seen on her dad's face before. His eyes sparkled at her now as she said it.

"Actually, Jett, there *is* something I want to discover. And also something I want *you* to discover. But first I have a question for you." He paused for a moment, waiting for her to make eye contact.

"Honey, do you want a dog?"

Jett felt frozen in time. *What*?!? Elation flooded through her. Had he really just said that? She wished she could rewind time and play that moment again.

Sure, he was witnessing the shock register on not only her face but all over her body, Jett realized she had to get a handle on her system or it might overload. She might even blackout. Ugh, not now! Jett plopped down into a chair and held onto the arm rails. She gripped them tightly. "Of course I want a puppy!"

Daddio smiled. "Okay, honey. But not a puppy. A dog. I need to know if you want a dog—a Gus or Yoda—of your very own."

Jett was back on her feet in an instant. "Really? Like really, *really*?" Jumping and waving her arms up and down, she looked like a baby bird trying to take flight. "Daddio! YES, I want a dog! Do I get to help pick? A boy or a girl? Oh-my-gosh! Are you freaking kidding me with this? DO. I. WANT. A. DOG?"

She ran around the desk that had been separating them

and tackled him with the biggest hug in recent history. "How did you even know? Is Mother okay with this? Have you confirmed and reconfirmed with her—maybe gotten it on tape or in writing? Something binding so she can't change her mind. Can we go right now?" Jett pulled away and started toward the door, tugging at his hand.

"Wait a minute. Wait a minute-," Daddio chuckled, a grin lighting up his face. When he didn't make any move to depart, Jett deflated slightly and looked back at him expectantly. He pointed her back to her chair, and hesitantly, she sat.

"Kiddo, I didn't mean right this minute," he said gently. "I'll take that as a yes, but it's gonna take time. There are things I need to tell you. And there are things I don't know that I need you to tell me. Are you up for figuring this out together?"

Jett just nodded wordlessly. She figured the sooner he finished speaking, the sooner they could go.

Daddio took a deep, audible breath and looked down at the desk. "I'm glad we cleared that up," he said. When he shifted his gaze back to her, he looked composed, but also a little concerned. Jett wondered what that was about.

"Honey, when I saw you with Gus at the Learning Lodge, I saw how quickly you two loved each other." Jett nodded and smiled at the memory. Drawing another deep breath, he continued. "Gus is a pretty special dog. You know that, right? He's not like… like just a dog that someone plopped down at the Lodge and boom! Magic. Gus knew what to do and how to act and how to help because he was trained and evaluated and given options to work or to be a pet without a specific purpose. Until they were sure he wanted the life of a facility dog, Gus had other options. Do you know what that means?"

Jett continued nodding, still hoping to wrap this up quickly, but then she realized that, no, she didn't know what Daddio meant.

"Tell me more, please. What do you mean, a 'facility dog'? Is that what Yoda will be? He's away at school getting training to help someone, but Ben told me he may not pass. He may become a home dog instead. Is that what you mean?" She thought she was connecting the dots, but then a new concern invaded her freshly settled mind. "Are you telling me I'm going back to live at the Lodge? Like—forever?"

"Oh, NO, Jett! No, not at all, sweetheart," he said, reaching for her hand and giving it a squeeze. "No, that time without you was the hardest period of my life. Even harder than when you were here but not speaking, with me sleeping in the hallway to keep you safe." He wiped a hand down his face anxiously. "Oh, kiddo. I only meant—do you want a dog of your own, like a service dog? Do you even know what that means exactly?"

Relieved she wasn't being sent away for good, Jett shook her head, trying in vain to clear the confusion.

"I want a dog for sure, but a service dog? Aren't those dogs for people who need special help, like people who can't hear or see or something? What would I need a dog like that for?"

Jett looked into her dad's face and saw his tenderness, his concern that he may not say whatever he had to say in a way that would connect with her.

"Bug, I'm so relieved you even know what service dogs are," he said. "I know you haven't seen many and I know this is probably weird for you. But did you know there are service dogs for people with…"

He struggled for a moment. "People with your brain type? There are service dogs for all kinds of things that people need help with, like monitoring their blood sugar levels and cardiac episodes and seizures and… and stuff."

"Yeah, but Dad, I don't have any of those things," she said. "My brain is fantastic! It may be wired differently, but still, it works great. I can see and hear, there's nothing wrong with my heart, I've never had a seizure, and my blood doesn't even get to have sugar very often. Mother makes sure of that. I'm not like any of those people."

She saw that Daddio was watching her carefully. He had said her "brain type." Maybe someone with a brain injury needed a specially trained dog, but not her. He wasn't making sense.

Daddio pursed his lips, considering how to proceed.

"Yep, Jett. You are totally 100 percent right. You have a fantastic brain. I wouldn't want it any other way. Do you know how proud I am of you?"

Yes, she knew. But she eyed him cautiously as she nodded.

"You are also a little bit wrong here, kiddo. You *are* like them." He put a hand to his chest. "I am like them. We are all like them. And while you and I can see and hear, we each have things that are harder for us. Some are harder than others. Does that make sense?"

Jett shrugged, still feeling off balance. "But what about service dogs? I don't know anyone who has one and if we all have things that are hard for us..."

He stopped her with a quick wave of the hand.

"Well, kiddo, that's where my research comes in. I started by calling Sylvia at the Lodge and asking if Gus helped you. I asked her to explain it to me. She said the first thing she noticed was that he gave you a safe place where you felt you could speak again." His voice broke a little and he stopped to clear his throat. "She wasn't even sure it was a feeling. Was it, Doodlebug? Did you feel you could speak to Gus but you couldn't speak to anyone else?"

Jett felt helpless as she struggled to answer. "It just happened. I swear. It wasn't conscious. It just happened."

He rushed to reassure her. "I'm not upset with you, honey. I just want to understand. No one trained Gus specifically for you, but he still helped. He chose to. Sylvia said he knew when you were getting anxious and would lean into you. He'd change his body position when you were super excited and slapping your thighs. She said you would stop immediately and refocus. Did you know that?"

Jett shook her head. She hadn't noticed any of that.

"She also told me that Gus helped you engage with people on a whole new level, speaking to others first. Usually, you were petting Gus at the same time." He looked into her eyes. "I've never seen you start a conversation. Did Gus really have something to do with that?"

Jett shrugged again. She didn't know.

"Well, what I do know is *if* you need help on a fairly regular basis, and *if* a dog could help you—maybe even improve your independence and quality of life—I'm all for it," he said. He reached into a drawer and took out a sheet of paper. "There are lists of tasks that service dogs can help with, and I think some apply to you. It's okay to tell me what you find difficult, especially because we'll find solutions. So—*Do* you think you need help, maybe with some of these?"

She glanced at the long list and shrugged. She picked it up and peered closer. How many did you need to qualify as deserving help? Was that even how it worked? "I don't know. Maybe? Sometimes?"

Daddio cocked his head and watched her silently, waiting. As Jett looked at the list, she thought about all the recent times she wanted to just "get it", to just fit in. She met his gaze. "So, just between us?"

Her Dad crossed his arms but didn't speak. He knew this was a big moment.

"It can be really exhausting being me, trying to sort out how to respond to everything like everyone else does. And sometimes I can't," she said. "Sometimes I'm too tired or stressed or acting in ways others just... don't—and I don't even know it! Can a dog help with that? Because if so, I want one. But I only want a dog who can go with me everywhere, if they can do that. *Can* they do that, help with things on the list *and* go everywhere? Is that a service dog?"

Daddio tapped the piece of paper, nodding. "Short answer: Yes. I think so. I don't know all the details, but some service dogs can be specially task-trained to help their partner do things that other people don't even have to think about." He swallowed hard and fixed her with a determined look. "Do you think that's you? Should we try?"

She twisted her fingers together, studying them as she puzzled through it. There were clues every single day that she was not typical. But how would that qualify her for a service dog? What could a dog do to help?

"Daddio, I don't know," she admitted with a sigh. "I mean, I am who I am every day. And every day I adjust as best I can to how the world needs me to be so that people can think I'm like everyone else. But it's so exhausting and sometimes I just can't. You know? Sometimes, I just don't act like my friends or like you and Mom. But I don't see how a dog could help."

Her dad let out the breath he had been holding. He stood up and started to pace.

"Wow, kiddo. You blow me away with your self-knowledge," he said. "But that's what I thought, too. So I talked to this organization that trains dogs to help people with your specific brain type and I put you on the waitlist, just in case that was your answer. This type of training typically takes about two years, but they have pups already working on training before they have partners, so it may not be that long. It also depends on the other people in line before you. Sometimes they don't have a match yet but there's a dog available. That dog could be *your* match. Does that make sense?" Joe frowned and pinched his eyebrows together with his right hand. "It's complicated."

It was Jett's turn to be blown away. She noticed him eyeing her surreptitiously, just as Sam and Andy sometimes did. What were they looking for?

"So you're telling me you've found a place that could train—specifically *for me*—my own Gus or Yoda. Am I hearing you right?"

"Yes, Love Bug, that's what I'm telling you. Oof—" Jett met him in the middle of the office, where he had been pacing and knocked the air out of his lungs with the force of her hug.

He held her gently by the shoulders and got serious again. "There's a long list and we're just at the beginning of the process, kiddo," he warned. "You have to go through assessments and interviews and training, too. But *someday*, you could have your own Gus or Yoda."

He stepped back to the desk and opened another drawer as he continued. "There's a lot of prep work involved, starting now. I need you to figure out where you need help."

Joe Harper handed a small, brightly colored journal to his daughter. "Start by keeping a diary. Track your days so you know what would make life easier. The dog would not only be your companion and aide, but also your responsibility. You'll have to deal with people will wonder why *you* have a dog with you everywhere and I know your Mom will be concerned about how their questions and attitudes will affect you. So I need you to make a list of how you want to be helped."

Jett stood still in the middle of the room where he had left her. Her eyes started to leak but she refused to acknowledge that. She nodded solemnly. "I can do that. But can we do it together? Can you help me sort it all out if I share with you about my days?"

Jett thought his voice sounded funny. He cleared his throat. "Um, sure, kiddo. I love you. It would be my honor and my pleasure to help you sort this out." He laughed softly. "Don't worry about your mother. She'll adjust when we tell her. But let's wait until we have all the supporting arguments lined up. Agreed? I think that will be soon enough."

Jett hugged him a little tighter. "Thanks, my Daddio. Thanks for thinking of this. I promise I will take care of the dog. I promise."

Smiling, Jett practically danced out of the room. She was getting her own Yoda-Gus.

3

FINALLY! THE FIRST day of school and Jett couldn't be more excited. She arrived early to get in a voice lesson with Sam before the school year "officially" began. Sam had been teaching Jett how to sing all summer, and now she couldn't wait to show Sam how much she had learned.

The heart of Presidio Prep's music hall was currently beating to lilting tones and tangible laughter. Other people must already be here. When Jett saw Sam, she waved. Sam must surely be her Bestie.

"Hey, Jett."

"Hey, Sam. Are you excited about today? I can hardly wait!"

Eyes twinkling, Sam grinned a worn smile, pocketing Jett's payment for the lesson as they got started. "Okay, show me what you got."

Jett threw down her pack, planted her feet, bent her knees and squared her shoulders. She was ready.

"Breathe, Jett. Breathe."

Jett huffed, and Sam laughed. She coaxed Jett into singing a few runs and into expressing herself through the notes. Jett thought they were having glorious fun, even though that last bit had been tricky.

"Sing it again, Sam?" Jett grinned. She was so clever. Did Sam catch her reference? Her grin broadened. "How about you sing it and then I'll try." Body rocking back and forth, Jett waited for Sam to sing, but it wasn't what she expected.Sam didn't continue with their vocal exercises and she didn't sing the song they'd been working on together.

Instead, she closed her eyes, took a deep breath, and began. When the last note left the air, she opened her eyes. The song had been slow and soulful and entirely her own, a common song sung the world over but a version unimagined by anyone else.

Jett swayed in place, eyes closed, tears falling, memorizing the moment. "Sam! That was the best rendition of 'Happy Birthday' ever! Thanks for that. What a gift! And even though it was my birthday a couple of days ago, I have been working on a surprise for you, too. I learned a song all on my own and I want to sing it for you, or at least try."

Jett stopped, suddenly wondering if this was a good idea after all. She felt shy. Quite aware her singing was not at Sam's level, she hoped the effort, the trying, would be recognized. That's what really mattered, right? She so wanted to take what Sam had taught her and give back to her in this way. Jett had spent so much time working on this surprise for her Best Friend that she now wondered which smile would light Sam's face. She had been loving her lessons with Sam and hoped for more.

After a moment, she took a deep breath, closed her eyes, and opened her mouth. She also opened her heart, feeling vulnerable in her sharing. When Jett finished singing, she opened her eyes. She was ready to meet Sam's smile with a grin of her own, but it wasn't there. Sam actually looked angry. Jett squinted. Was she seeing this correctly? Her face fell. She stayed silent, waiting for a clue about what might have gone wrong.

"NO!" Sam bellowed. "This isn't happening. Seriously, Jett? Did you and Miya come up with this? I can't even. I just—" Sam shook her head violently, as if she were trying to forget what she'd just heard.

Jett held up her hands, trying to fend off the explosion of anger, confused beyond her limit. "Sam, I don't know what you mean. I'm guessing you didn't like my singing, but do you know this song? It's 'Be Kind' by Zak Abel. I can send you a link. Do you want me to try again? Maybe I can do a better job."

"No. You've done enough already." Sam gathered up her things. "This was a mistake, an epic fail. Damn it. I don't know what I was thinking." She reached into her pocket. "Here, Jett. Take your money. I'm done. No more lessons. I can't listen to you anymore."

Jett froze. The money fluttered to the ground as Sam left. What the hell just happened? She went over every note and every phrase she had sung. She hadn't fumbled and she didn't think she was off key. Why had Sam gotten so angry?

She fumbled in her backpack and pulled out her phone. Quickly, she replayed the original artist's version of the song, listening carefully. She couldn't hear anything that she might have done wrong. And Sam's rejecting the money for the lesson confused her even more. Was she implying the entire summer had been a mistake or just her trying this song?

An alarm went off, and Jett looked back at her phone. She groaned; she had to go right now. If she didn't hurry, she would be late to her first Foundations class as a sophomore. Today was turning into a disaster, just like her song.

JETT FELT THE sun-kissed warmth of late summer dance across her skin as she ran across campus. She was late. It was her first class, on her first day of her second year at Presidio Prep and she was late. She hated being late. Why had Sam run off without her, without even a warning that time was growing short? Sam's anger couldn't *entirely* be about her inability to sing. What was she missing?

She burst into Ms. Diaz's room with little grace and a lot of noise. Jett cringed at the door's unexpected bang, even though she was the one who flung it open. Somehow, she didn't expect the impact.

"Ho ho! Look who's here everybody! My Manita is making an entrance today!" Carlos clapped to draw attention to himself while Jett landed in the last seat in their group. Sam glared at her as Carlos flung his arms wide and turned around to ensure everyone saw him.

She looked at her teammates, at her first friends. The Core5 was all there, but Sam had pushed her seat slightly outside their usual circle. Jett looked around the room, wondering whether the other groups were as close. They were all gathered in their teams. Did anyone know what was going on yet?

Ms. Diaz answered her unspoken question. "Good morning, everyone! Soon enough, you will start putting in great effort on your sophomore projects. I like to call it the 'sophomore surprise' and you will learn more about it later." She rubbed her hands together and did a quick turn as she paced at the front of the class. "Right now, though, it's important for you to catch up with your team members. You will be working closely together again and it's important you leave no one behind. Last year, we learned how to be loving people and today I expect you to practice that. Work together. Questions?"

A few feet shuffled in the quiet, but otherwise the room was silent. "Aaaaand—that's it for now! By the way, if you've got a team member missing, let me know so I can track their absence. Otherwise, get to it! Learn more about your teammates and their summers!" She clapped twice and turned back to her desk. Jett watched Ms. Diaz pick up a colorful mug and put it to her lips. She wondered how the teacher would spend the hour.

When Jett refocused on her Core5, she saw that Sam was looking down, furiously texting and ignoring everyone.

Surprisingly—or then again, maybe not—Ruby was the first to address Sam's breach of etiquette. "Um—hello!" She dipped her head in front of Sam's phone. Sam acknowledged Ruby with a pronounced growl. Ruby just smirked. "We're in this together, right? That means you need to be here in real life. We need to catch up on everyone's summer, even yours." Ruby put her hands on her hips and looked around at the Core5. "Who's going first? Andy, is it you? You with the updated look, wearing trendy new glasses. Are you now the poster-boy for geek chic?"

Andy shrugged as the color rose on the back of his neck. He fidgeted uncomfortably and looked down as Jett looked down. She stole a peek and he *was* wearing new glasses. Huh. Leave it to Ruby to notice.

Sam watched Ruby warily, and Carlos grinned. Ruby pointed to him. "Okay, lover boy. You start us off." She folded her arms and leaned back in her seat. "How was *your* summer?"

"Mine was *great*!" Carlos enthused. "I was team captain! We won the summer league, and I scored the most points!

And of course, I was the best player. I even won an award for that! Also, I ate the best food! I went to all the food truck things my Papa scheduled for us. You should have heard some of the music. Did you know there are food truck events every single night? It's like a big party!" He gestured around the circle. "You should all come! Seriously. We need to do that when my Papá and Mamá are there. They already talk like you're *familia*." He looked expectantly at his teammates.

Jett didn't know whether it was for confirmation that they would come to a food truck party or whether he was looking for the next summer report.

Hearing nothing, he turned to Ruby. "Who's next, Linda?"

Ruby smirked. "I can top that, but maybe we should let the boys go first. Andy? Your turn."

Andy pulled in his long legs, hiding his colorful socks and sitting up straighter as he pushed his glasses up on the bridge of his nose. He cleared his throat nervously.

"Um—okay. My summer was full of family and mostly about our big adventure going back to Gujarat to see even *more* family," he said. "My cousin's wedding took an entire week. It was so colorful and festive!"

He grinned over at Carlos. "I ate a whole lot, too. The food was so good! I'm going to ask my Dadi to make some for all of you to try." Then he looked at Jett. "Also, I got a text from Jett over the summer, but no one else. Thank you, Jett."

"Me too!" Carlos said. "Did you text everyone in our group, Jett?"

"She didn't text *me*," Ruby huffed. She looked at Sam. "Did she text you?" When Sam nodded, Ruby plastered on a class 10 pout.

Jett was surprised. Was she supposed to text half-friends too? Huh. She'd have to remember that.

"Not like it really mattered to me," Ruby said, turning pointedly away from Jett. "I was super busy working on the 'teens who save the world' campaign and all, so I don't know if I would have seen the text had she bothered to send one. I spent *most* of the summer in front of the cameras and giving interviews and doing social justice work—like literally changing the world." She turned to Sam. "What did you do?"

Sam rolled her eyes. "I didn't win soccer awards. I didn't go to a fancy wedding on the opposite side of the globe. I didn't save the world," she said, folding her arms to mirror Ruby's posture. "Pretty much, I spent the summer just being *normal*." Sam focused dagger eyes on Jett, who knew better than to talk about their singing lessons.

It was Jett's turn now, but she was torn about what to say. Could she make Sam feel important by bringing up 'Hamilton' or would that send her further down her negative spiral?

She knit her hands together on top of her desk and focused on them. "I too had a completely normal summer. I mean, nothing was *typical*, but it sure was *normal*."

She grinned at her own cleverness and how she had copied Sam to ensure she felt supported. Jett hoped Sam had gotten her secret message, but when she saw Sam's glare, Jett felt deflated.

Sam looked ready to pounce. "Really, Jett?" she snarled. "You think copying me will *finally* make you cool? Guess again. You got that wrong, too. It doesn't. It just makes you look stupid and insecure." Sam began shoving her things into her messenger bag and got up to leave.

Realizing Sam was leaving class early, Jett was desperate to let Sam know she was here for her. She was *still* her best friend, after all.

Jett reached out and put her hand on Sam's forearm, but Sam shook her off. Jett tried again. She grabbed Sam's hand and gave it a squeeze before Sam yanked out of her grasp. Jett felt the withdrawal like a slap to her face. She watched Sam walk out of class and felt a lone tear run down her face.

At Sam's abrupt departure, Ms. Diaz looked up but didn't stop her.

Ruby watched in fascination. "Ooh! So, it's like that, is it? You like Sam."

Jett swallowed hard and nodded.

Ruby moved in for the kill. "I mean you *like*–like her, right?"

Jett just nodded again and wiped the tear from her cheek.

Carlos came over and put his arm around her. "I'm sorry. I didn't know," he said soothingly. "You know you can tell me, right?"

Jett looked up at him, then into Andy's eyes, which looked especially sad.

Andy offered her a small smile. "Me, too, Jett. I like her, too."

She reached for his hand and they stayed connected for a moment, Carlos, Jett, and Andy. Ruby wasn't invited, and Jett was glad. After all, Ruby wasn't an everywhere friend. She was a half-friend, if *that*. No, *not* that. Jett thought Ruby was maybe a *quarter*-friend.

And Sam was nowhere to be seen.

4

THAT AFTERNOON ON her way to meet with Presidio Prep's counselor, Dr. Williams, Jett skipped down the sidewalk. She was grateful for their standing weekly appointment. She had many things to discuss this afternoon, not the least of which was Sam's strange behavior and why her teammates thought her liking Sam was such a big deal. Weren't friends supposed to not only like but also love each other? She knocked lightly on the doorframe and entered Dr. Williams' office.

"Good afternoon, Jett!" he said, rising from his desk with a smile. "Come in, come in. I'm glad to see you. Tell me how the beginning of the new school year is treating you."

Jett waved a quick greeting as she sat down across from him. "Hi, Dr. W. How's your day going?" She fiddled with the straps on her Spiketus Rex; it was such a comfort to still be carrying her signature backpack. Did her uncle, who gave it to her, know she was still sporting it a year later? She would have to drop him a text to be sure he did.

never knew where to start when she was trying to unravel a problem. Should she go back to *Hamilton* and her promise to Miya, or should she skip to Sam walking out on her twice now? It was all so confusing! She saw Dr. W studying her intently. Wouldn't it be so much easier if he could pull the information out of her head Borg-style? For the first time in her life, she wished she was Borg.

"Honestly, Dr. W, I don't know where to begin," she admitted. "What would you like to know?"

Dr. W nodded as if that was what he had expected. "It does sound pretty confusing," he agreed. "Do you know what Ruby meant when she asked if you 'like-like' Sam, and why the rest of your Core5 acted like that was a big deal?"

"It made no sense to me," she said, shaking her head. "I thought liking each other was part of being friends. It is, isn't it?"

"Yes, liking each other is part of being friends," Dr. W said, smiling at her. "But when Ruby used the specific term 'like-like,' she meant romantically. She was asking if you had amorous or lustful feelings for Sam. When you said yes, I think that took the rest of the team by surprise. I think—"

"Wait—what?" Jett interjected. "That doesn't even make sense! 'Like-like' means romantic like? That's ridiculous! And how come everyone else knew that and I didn't? Do they have a different dictionary I need to get? Besides, what's wrong with like-liking Sam, if I did? I don't actually have romantic feelings for her. I'm too busy just trying to keep up with friendship feelings for so many people. But if I did, why would that be such a big deal? Or is it because she stormed out? Isn't it logical I would be upset about that? Shouldn't they all be? Doesn't that make *more* sense?"

This was so exasperating! Relationship stuff was a lot harder than formulas and data. At least numbers and hard facts were predictable. She closed her eyes, trying to steady her breathing.

When she opened them, she saw Dr. W giving her a kindly, understanding look. "Once again, you've proven how brilliant you are," he reassured her. "Relationships and definitions and understanding what others mean are way trickier than formulas for you, aren't they?"

"Aren't they for everybody?" asked Jett.

Dr. W chewed the inside of his cheek for a moment, like he was trying to sort out how to say what he needed to say.

"Well, Jett. The honest answer is no," he said sympathetically. "That doesn't mean people don't have misunderstandings, but communicating isn't as hard as math for most people. It simply is harder for you, and I'm sorry for that."

He paused for a long sip from the mug on his desk, considering. "I think it's because you are what I like to call a deep thinker. One of your superpowers is consideration. Not everyone is as considerate as you are. So many people make assumptions, but you question and consider. That means you understand even *better* when you're on the right track, but it also means that you miss things that others get right away."

Taking a deep breath, he lightly rapped his knuckles on the desk. "If I sound like I'm talking in riddles today, forgive me. I'm probably making no sense to you. Let me try again."

He held up a finger. "One: A dog could help you with some things that would allow you to spend more time sorting through complex problems that others don't even recognize as an issue." Up came a second finger. "Two: Most people don't recognize the complexities of communication because they assume their biases and definitions are pretty universal, whereas you are smart enough to avoid that trap." And now a third finger joined the first two. "And three: that makes you different. It makes you normal, not typical."

He paused for a moment, taking another sip from his mug. "Is that clear as mud? Do you want to talk about how to clear up the misunderstandings with your Core5, or what to do about Sam, or what a dog could possibly do for you? Where do we go next, Jett Harper? I'm at your disposal."

Jett felt dizzy from the revelations of the last few minutes. She shook her head wearily. "I'm sorry, Dr. W. I'm actually pretty tired now. You've given me a lot to consider. Can I get a pass to go take a nap? Maybe which problem to solve or topic to discuss will be apparent after I sleep a bit."

He smiled and gestured toward the opposite side of his office. "All right then. You could use my favorite spot in that chair with a blanket and pillow by the window. I can go next door to the conference room and work from there. Come get me when you're ready to talk or if you're going to leave."

Jett just nodded. That sounded perfect.

JETT WOKE UP half an hour later filled with resolve. As soon as she found Dr. W next door reading, she started talking. "I'm feeling better and I think I know which way I want to go." She explained her thought process on the walk back into his office.

"I want to talk about Sam. I mean, not *about* her, like gossip, but about me and how I relate to Sam, since two of our three discussion options are really about Sam."

She stopped, studying her counselor intently. "What's the statute of limitations for secrets? You won't tell anyone else what I tell you, right?"

The man crossed his heart with his long fingers. "I won't tell anyone anything without us first having a discussion about it and usually not even then—not unless someone is a danger to themselves or to others. And you *definitely* are not."

Satisfied, she continued. "Okay. Here's the deal. Sam

is sad. Like, really, really sad, and it's affecting her actions and maybe even how she's thinking." Now that she had decided what to talk about, her words came out in a rush. "I've been trying to get her to talk to me, but she just won't. And today she was mean to me—twice!—and I don't know what to do. I tried to reach out to her, but *that* totally backfired."

Jett rolled her eyes at the memory. "I know I'll have to address that issue soon, but Sam herself is more important than that right now. I just don't know what I'm supposed to do. How do I let her know I'm her best friend if she won't let me?"

Both Jett and Dr. W sighed heavily at the same time. They looked at each other silently, the air in the room weighted with their thoughts.

Dr. W sighed again, propping his elbows on his desk and lacing his fingers together. "Jett, that is a problem. I don't have a formula for you to solve. Here's what I do know: Friends are loyal, even when they hit a disconnect. They give each other space to feel whatever they're going to feel while they wait for reconnection. From what you say, it sounds like Sam is really hurting a lot. Would you like me to speak with her? I could have her come to my office, if you think that would help."

Jett quickly put up her hands and shook her head. "She might think I told you things, private things, and I would hate to lose my first every day, every where best friend."

Dr. W nodded thoughtfully. "You're right. So here's what I would do if I were you. I would try to speak to her in her love language. I'd write her a note as well, even if words aren't her top language, just so she has a physical reminder of how much she means to you. Write to her. Let her know you care and show her by communicating in a way that she can hear."

The tension that had been pushing Jett's shoulders up around her ears began to ease away. They dropped slowly as she nodded her agreement. "Thanks! I do think that will help. I'll try it. Can you suggest any backup plans?"

He sighed again. "I'm sorry, but the only viable backup plan is time," he said, giving her a rueful smile. "All you can do is remind her that you're available and you care. Then you have to give her time. I can't help but think she'll come around. You two are part of the same Core5 team. It's not like you won't be interacting and seeing each other. Be patient and she will see you as you are: Jett Harper, the *best* best friend."

Jett smiled and reached to collect her things, nodding as she committed his words to memory. She had a plan. She would be Sam's best best friend, just as the doctor counseled.

5

FOUNDATIONS, THE INTEGRAL social studies program for Presidio Prep, was housed down a busy corridor in the main building. Every student had to pass through the Hall of Fame and its wall of achievements. Mementos, trophies, and corresponding photos marked the way to class. Because Jett's Core5 had won the Freshman Faire last year, their photo held a central place of honor—smack dab in the center of the largest display case. This constant reminder of last year's project made her feel so proud. They had all come so far. The work had paid off, including a special field trip to Safari West, a private zoo 60 miles north of their campus. She certainly wanted to go there again, but more than that, she wanted her team to win the Sophomore Grand Prize. Could they prove their prowess two years in a row? The first step would be choosing the right focus and that could be tricky.

Today, each team member would present their own idea for a potential theme. Then, as a team, they would decide which idea to bring forth for their focus. Jett couldn't wait to see what everyone thought up, especially her best friend, Sam.

Ms. Diaz interrupted her thoughts. "Good morning, sophomores! Today is the day! Are you ready? It's Pick. Your. Focus!" She announced this with all the enthusiasm of a game-show host, rounding it off with an imitation of clapping and cheering from a live audience. "Does anyone have an example they'd like to share? Anyone? Anyone?"

All 30 students stared mutely back at her.

Undaunted, Ms. Diaz carried on with her game show persona.

"To get your creativity going, I'll tell you that last year's winning team focused on imagination. While a quotation from Einstein inspired them, I'm inspired by something George S. Patton said: 'Never tell people how to do things. Tell them what to do and they will surprise you with their ingenuity.'"

She peered expectantly around at them. "I will not tell you how to do it, but what I want you to do is to identify what you're passionate about, enough to develop ingenuity. Anyone need a definition?"

Around the room, a few hands went up while others quickly grabbed their phones and started tapping for answers. When Andy raised his hand, she beckoned toward him with a hand that sported brightly polished nails in an array of colors.

"What've you got for us?"

Andy squared his shoulders, peering at his phone as he cleared his throat. "The Macmillan Dictionary defines ingenuity as 'ability to solve problems in clever ways,' and the Oxford Dictionary says 'the quality of being clever, original, and inventive,' so I think the main thing you're asking for is for us to solve something in a creative or original way." He looked up from his phone. "Have I got that right?"

Ms. Diaz nodded as she bowed to him with a flourish. "Well done, Mr. Katiya, well done."

She opened her arms wide toward the class. "He's got that exactly right. I want you all to be ingenious." To stave off some of the puzzled expressions that painted their faces, she rushed to clarify. "This year, I want you to work together as a team on one inspiration. Make the result count. Solve something. Create something. Think outside the box and use your ingenuity. Each team will develop only one idea over the entire school year, so make sure you all agree on which concept that should be. Are you ready to sort that out?" After a quick drum roll of her fingers on the nearest desk, Ms. Diaz gesticulated wildly. "Okay? Ready. Set. Go!"

She clapped her hands. Groups moved quickly into tighter huddles and a low hum of excitement charged the air. If only this enthusiasm could be harnessed into productive energy, Jett thought, they could fuel the entire Presidio, maybe all of San Francisco.

"Are you guys ready?" she asked as her Core5 nodded eagerly. Jett was glad to see a smile on Sam's face. "Who wants to go first?"

Carlos' hand shot up in the air. "Pick me, Manita! I want to go first. I want to talk about The Winning!" Waiting scarcely a beat for her nod, he launched into his pitch, keeping the Core5 entertained the whole time. He wrapped up with a proud flourish. "So, that's my idea. We're all winners here. How do we teach others to be winners like us? Let's spend the year using our *ingenuity* to find out."

Arms folded across his chest, Carlos nodded like the group had already decided to pursue his idea. Jett tried not to laugh. She could tell by the way he beamed that he was proud of his idea and his presentation. She was glad Carlos was her first everywhere friend.

Carlos turned his entire body towards Andy. He gestured with both hands, keeping his pointer fingers extended like guns. With a broad smile and curt nod of encouragement, the team knew who was up next, and four pairs of eyes turned their focus on Andy.

He drew them into his thoughts. "Community is key. We need to work together and take care of each other. We should contribute our excess resources to taking care of those who aren't as fortunate. I'd like for us to explore more about how to *be* a better community."

Ruby nodded even as the patronizing smile she wore spoke a different message. She jumped right in. "That's great, boys. Winning and community are both important concepts. But I think we ought to focus on individual impact. We need people to recognize that what they do matters; their efforts are seen, and that should motivate them to do better."

Sam rolled her eyes at Ruby. Right leg jogging up and down, Sam obviously couldn't wait another minute to speak. She looked ready to spring, and indeed she did. Passionately. "What about survival? I mean, I know you all—I mean, *we* don't know much about what it takes to survive in the *real* world, but wouldn't it be cool if we did? Wouldn't it be cool to know what it took to live on your own, right now, if you had to?"

Sam jumped up and started pacing around the group. As she walked around behind them, each turned to watch her. She made eye contact with each one. "What would you do? How would you avoid getting caught up in the system so you could control your own schedule and be in charge of your own life? What would you do to keep going to this fancy school and whatever? Where would you live? How would you get food? What would it take to make it through each day?"

Hands knotted, arms taught, wrists held rigidly like she was wearing handcuffs, Sam shook her head. "This isn't even a fair system. It's rigged for the *rich*. People struggling just to survive can't even *dream* about what we take for granted here every day. So that's what I want to know. How do you thrive when you need to survive? I think it's an important question for us to answer and our *ingenuity* is key to figuring it out."

Everyone was silent as the gears turned in their minds. The air grew heavy as they weighed scenarios and possibilities of Sam's challenge. Sam had presented... Sam. She had just dropped a serious, real topic into the middle of their little collective and they weren't sure they were equipped to handle it. When no one had spoken for so long that the silence became a voice unto itself, Jett spoke up.

"Okay, so we have winning, community, individual impact, and survival to consider so far. I'm wondering if we're ready to vote. Anyone have any last-minute points for us to consider?"

Andy raised his hand. "Don't you have a theme for us to consider, Jett?"

She shook her head. "Not really. I wanted to talk about the being normal, but *I* think we already have enough to think about."

The group debated their next step. Andy spelled out a plan for making community a focus and what they might do to study the subject. Ruby advocated for developing guidelines around how to be an influencer with more individual impact; she was, of course, prepared to lead the project. Carlos and Sam took turns throwing out ideas to entice people to their side. As the debate died down, they grew anxious, knowing that only one concept would be chosen.

"All right, crew, let's vote," Jett said. "Remember that you can't vote for your own idea and there's always next year. And keep in mind that maybe we could combine the top two if they tie?" Internally, she shrugged. Who knew what would happen next year? She didn't want to put people on the spot. She breathed with relief as she came up with a solution. Reaching into her backpack, she took out notecards and handed them around the circle. "Everyone, write down what you would like to learn together this year. Fold it over and hand it to me. Andy, you tally the votes. Ready?"

They were.

Jett was a little surprised to learn that, of the five votes, the team was split between all the ideas except "individual impact." That was the only concept to be mentioned by two team members. She felt bad that Sam's idea had received no votes. Even her idea about being normal, which she herself had vetoed, had gotten a vote of support. Should she have chosen Sam's idea because she wanted to be a better best friend? Or should she vote as she did, for the idea she thought could win the competition? If she changed her vote, then no one would win... Gah! She was glad they had cast their votes privately and no one would know who had chosen what. She felt like a traitor, but was also glad to know her vote mattered.

Ruby smirked when she realized her idea had been chosen. "Ha! I knew it! I *knew* you all secretly want to be me! Great choice to the two who made this happen. Care to fess up?" The team peered around the circle, trying to divine who had supported what.

"Ummm... who did this to us?" Sam said with an edge in her voice. "No. Really—" She was beginning to smoulder. Arms crossed protectively over her chest, she breathed heavily. Finally, she looked at Jett. "Really? *You* didn't even vote for me? After acting like we are actually friends or... or something? I mean, I thought we stood up for each other! I thought I could *at least* count on *you* to vote for me. But you didn't. Nope. No. Just no. I know you didn't because NO ONE voted for me."

Throwing a look of disgust around the circle, she stood and gathered up her things. When her hands were full, she glared at the group. "You're all Ruby lackeys. That's what you've chosen over real life. Over *real* situations that people have to work through every day." She started nodding. "I get it. It's not you. It doesn't affect you. It's not *your* real world. But what if it was?" And with that, Sam turned her back on all of them and left.

Jett's internal monologue stumbled. Wait a minute. What happened to *us*? It's not *us*. Right? Isn't that what Sam meant? When had it changed from us to you?

Abandoning her backpack, Jett sprinted after Sam. "Sam!" she called out. "Wait for me!" Heads turned to watch the drama, but she didn't care. She wondered what she could possibly say.

Outside the classroom, Sam rounded on her. "What? What do you want, Jett? I can't believe that just happened. My Grams told me to open up to the group with a really good—a really *real* idea. She said to talk about what's relevant so we can create what's possible. Well, she was wrong. She was wrong because there are many different kinds of real, aren't there? And mine just doesn't hold a candle to Ruby's."

As Jett felt her own throat swell, she saw tears fill Sam's eyes and heard raw pain in Sam's voice. She wondered what was causing such a strong reaction even as she felt it affect her body. This had to be about more than a class project.

Carefully, Jett swallowed the pain lodged in her throat. Her jaw flexed and she felt it all, this pivotal moment. She knew they could be exposing a hard and tender truth and hoped her friend would share more with her. "Tell me what's going on, Sam. Why are you so sad? Why are you so angry all the time? Is it because Miya's in LA?"

A tear slid down Sam's cheek as she shook her head. Jett scrunched her face, trying hard to understand. What was she missing?

"Is it a person? Is someone giving you a hard time? Do you need Andy to fight them? He's taking MMA, you know. I bet he'd fight for you." Sam's obvious pain made her ache inside. She wanted desperately to fix it. "If it's *me* making you feel this way, please know that I didn't mean to make you upset. I'm sorry I didn't vote for you. I thought we were voting for ideas, not people. If I knew we were voting for people, I would have chosen you over anyone else. I guess I messed up. Big time. What can I do now?"

Sam wasn't breathing like a frightened horse anymore. Her tears had spilled over, and she wasn't wiping them away. She was allowing them to flow, and Jett thought this was a good sign. Maybe Sam was about to open up to her and let her be her best friend. Maybe she could use Miya's suggestion and ask Sam about music to help get her started. But Sam had said there would be no more singing together. Trying to do it now wouldn't be right. Could she suggest it at another time? She would have to remember and look for the right opportunity. Jett tucked that internal note away.

Looking devastated, Sam just shook her head at Jett. "There's nothing you can do. *Nothing.* I just need—some time, okay? I mean, I need to figure all this stuff out and that's going to take some time. Okay? You got that?"

Jett just nodded. She got it. Sam needed time. She wanted to figure this stuff out. She... wait. What stuff? Should Jett ask or would her ignorance mark her as dumb like Sam had declared a few days ago? Jett didn't want to be dumb; she just wanted to understand. Jett wanted Sam to feel loved, and she certainly understood needing time. Jett could give her that. Dr. W had said to be patient.

"Okay, Sam. I can give you time. How much are you thinking? Want me to text you tonight?"

"Jett, if you have to ask before texting, the answer is always no. So—" She drew a deep breath, puffed out her cheeks, and blew it out through her lips. "I don't know how much time I'll need, but I may not be around for a little bit. Okay?" Sam started nodding, so Jett did too.

Inside her racing mind, Jett repeated what she'd just learned. She wanted to commit it all to memory. No texting if you had to ask and Sam needed time. Sam wouldn't be around, but it would only be a little bit. Jett didn't know how long that was exactly, but Sam had at least offered some clarification. She contemplated this as she watched Sam walk away. Rooted to the spot, she reminded herself that Sam had never lied to her. Dr. W had given her insight and Jett was following through with that, too. Sam would be gone for a little while, which also meant Sam would be back. Her timeline might not have been specific, but how bad could that be?

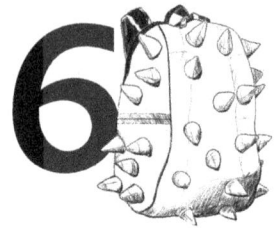

THE CAMPUS CAFE was humming with frenetic energy on this fog-laden morning. Warmth rushed out, inviting students in; the crowds grew. Jett wondered how her Core5 would stay focused. Still, she liked meeting here. It was one of her favorite places. When she was here by herself, she wore noise-canceling earbuds to control the extrasensory input. Even so, every time someone came near, she looked up. As her team approached, her anxiety ebbed. She could feel it in the slowing of her heart rate. Jett was used to being early and waiting for the others to arrive, but today everyone was late. It made waiting hard. When four of the five had gathered, drinks and snacks in front of them, Jett looked at the clock on the wall and then her phone. She peeked at Andy's socks. Blue with pizza. He must've been hungry when he chose them.

His voice broke through her internal chatter. "Where's Sam?"

Everyone looked around. No one had an answer. Jett was glad she wasn't the only one who noticed the absence. Sam was more than 25 minutes late. This was unusual, especially because she wasn't answering texts. What was going on?

Ruby looked directly at Jett and leaned forward. "You want to tell us where your honey is?" Her voice dripped with ridicule.

Blinking slowly, Jett stared back at Ruby. She blinked again. "First of all, I want to clear something up. Sam is my *best* friend. She is *not* my honey. She is her own honey. Also, I just learned what you meant by 'like-like' and I think it's silly—as if 'like' is a sliding scale from one like to like-like."

Jett rolled her eyes at this preposterous idea before pinning Ruby with a glare. "I also think you're out of line for even asking," she retorted. "I don't know where Sam is right now. She isn't answering my texts. She hasn't for days. And I haven't seen her since we were all in class together."

With eyebrows raised, Ruby rocked back like she'd been pushed. She looked surprised. Jett wondered if she had been too rude. She kept her chin raised and made herself look Ruby in the eye. She couldn't back down. Not now.

Carlos looked between the two of them. "Okay, okay. We got this. Sam is not your *novia*, and you don't know where she is. Right, Jett?"

Jett nodded, still holding Ruby's eyes, glare for glare.

He turned to Ruby. "Ruby, you need to remember not everyone uses language like you do, and my Manita speaks properly. Can I count on you to try not to confuse her? Can you be a little more—you know—nice to Jett? For me?" Carlos waited for a moment, as if he actually expected a reply. Then he put down his empty coffee mug and stood up.

Jett wondered what Ruby meant to imply when she broke off her glare, turning her head and looking away. She waited for Carlos to clarify the situation, but he didn't. Instead, he just silently shoved his hands into the front pockets of his jeans. Jeans today. He usually wore athletic wear. That was odd. She tried to catch his eye, but Carlos was busy studying the ground.

Andy intervened. "Okay, so we don't know where Sam is, but I'm sure she'll show up. She's just as reliable as the rest of us. This is a first. She was here while I was gone for Diwali last week. Right?" When Carlos, Ruby, *and* Jett all shook their heads 'no' in unison, Andy made a sound that reminded Jett of one her mother made when she was startled or surprised. "Huh, okay then. I'll text her. Carlos, you try too." He reached for his phone and quickly sent a message. When he was done, Andy stared down at his phone, while Carlos waved his in the air.

Jett wondered if they were expecting an immediate response. Then she had a thought. "Andy, did you hear from Sam recently?" He shook his head. "Can you look at your phone and see when was the last time?" She turned to the other two. "How about you? When was the last time Sam texted you?" Everyone pulled out their phones and began searching.

Ruby waved her phone like Carlos had and answered first. "Um, that would be a never for me. That girl is not in *my* contacts. I'm pretty sure we've never talked outside of the projects we've worked on together. Why would we?"

Jett was taken aback. She watched Carlos shake his head. His entire posture exuded disappointment. Andy frowned. Finally, Carlos weighed in. "It's been a while for me. We talked about a new game a few weeks ago. Does anyone know if she even knows about today?"

Jett felt increasingly anxious. She pulled at the hem of her shirt. "I told her about today, but she didn't respond. The last time I saw her was right after she walked away from our group. She told me she might not be around for a bit, but she said nothing about not answering texts." Jett began to fidget with the ends of her backpack and jiggle her right leg up and down.

Andy looked sheepish. "We text pretty regularly, but I got sidetracked with all the stuff I had coming up. Diwali is like my Christmas, but it lasts for five days and there's a lot of prep that goes into it. So—yeah. It's been a little while. It's been…" He looked at his watch and frowned. "13 days, actually. And usually she answers me pretty quickly." He looked at his phone and Jett could see him silently counting. "But now? Nothing." He looked up and met Jett's eyes. "Anyone else here worried?"

Ruby huffed as Jett and Carlos nodded in unison.

"Anyone have another way of contacting her? Do you know where she lives? I think I've seen her on the same train as me, but that could be a fluke. We've never actually talked about it."

The group fell silent.

Determination written all over his face, Andy stood up. "I think we should take this to Ms. Diaz to see if we can find something out. Maybe Sam is gone and forgot to tell *us,* but the teachers all know. She couldn't just be *gone*, you know?" He gathered his things. Everyone but Ruby followed suit.

Scornfully, Ruby protested their imminent departure. "But we're going to lose our table *and* these comfy chairs! Maybe I should just stay here. I can wait for you guys and text you if the loser bothers to show." Resolved, she nodded to herself. "I'll hold down the fort."

"There is no fort to hold down, but stay if you want," Jett said. "I'm not sure you should come, anyway. This seems like something people who care about Sam should do."

Andy and Carlos both coughed out a laugh. Andy covered his mouth with his hand while Carlos threw his hands up in a placating gesture. "Jett! Manita! Are you sure you meant that like it came out?"

Jett's increasing anxiety loosened her tongue. "What? I meant that Ruby should do what she wants. She wants to stay? Stay. She wants to come with us? Come. I just wanted her to know there was no fort to hold down, because—Duh! We're in a cafe! On campus! What did you think I said?"

Carlos and Andy looked at each other and grinned wider, mirroring their expressions as they shook their heads.

"Yeah, Jett. Okay." Carlos turned to Ruby. "She's right. Come if you want and stay here if you don't, but I, for one, don't know if we're coming back. We don't know where Sam is, but if we find out, I want to go see her. It's not cool to ghost your teammates."

Jett cocked her head at Carlos's peculiar expression but didn't have time to think about it. It was time to find Sam.

Ruby huffed again but stood up and they all left together. When they found Ms. Diaz, it was Ruby who spoke up. "Ms. Diaz, Sam isn't around. We're wondering if you know where she is right now. Was this some kind of excused absence and she didn't tell us?"

Andy jumped in. "Do you know when she'll be back?"

Ms. Diaz narrowed her eyes at them. "I was actually wondering if she told you guys but forgot to have her parents report in. So—you don't know, either?"

The group looked at each other with varying degrees of alarm, anxiety, and confusion on their faces. Carlos was the first to speak. "Um, no. We know nothing. Is there someone we should call? She isn't answering her texts."

With an increasingly deep furrow in her brow, Ms. Diaz nodded at them. "That *is* concerning. I'll look into it. In the meantime, you four can work on the project together and Sam can catch up when she returns. Yes?"

Ruby nodded confidently. She was the Lead, after all. "Thank you, Ms. Diaz. We can handle this. We're on track with our project and Sam can make it up to us when she appears again." Ruby motioned to them like they should all leave. When Jett hesitated, Ruby shooed her out the door insistently.

When they were safely out of earshot in the hallway, Jett exploded. "Wait. I don't understand. What just happened?"

Ruby gave her a withering look and went in for the kill. "You, dumbass. You just happened and you've caused our team to lose focus," she retorted. "Now we're sidetracked just because Sam is having a holiday! Seriously? So uncool. Sam probably isn't answering her phone because she's tired of your pestering. I would be. She doesn't answer to you."

Now she rounded on the boys. "She doesn't answer to you two either, Mutt and Jeff. I mean, come on! Do you really think your precious little chick Sam is in trouble? She's probably laughing at you guys right now."

That was too much. Carlos raised his voice as he took her on. "We care! That's what friends *do*, Ruby!" He looked at her with growing disgust. "Sam going missing, not answering texts and all, that's unusual. Of course we're worried. The real question is, why aren't you? Do you not have a heart? Like, for real—at all? The guys on my team told me you don't. Are they right?"

Jett was shocked. In all the time she had known him, Carlos only called Ruby "Linda." Jett remembered how she had worried that he suffered from a traumatic brain injury because of his consistent misidentification. She felt a bit wistful. Those were the days. Now they were facing *actual* problems. Probably. What if Ruby was right and Sam was just avoiding them all? But—what if she wasn't? Jett's heart dropped as she put the puzzle pieces together.

"Hold on a minute. Wait."

Three curious faces stared back at her. "Remember Sam's proposal for our project? What if that's a clue to her actual concern—her real life right now? I mean, she wanted to study survival, right? Like the *actual* 'how' of it, the 'what would you do' and things. What if she's really *not* okay?" Her muscles tensed at the thought. She noticed Andy's jaw muscle flex under his serious expression. Not really a pizza socks kind of day, after all.

She watched as each member of the Core5 absorbed her idea. She could see Ruby still thought she was overreacting, but maybe not as much as before. Carlos and Andy—especially Andy—both looked disturbed.

"What can we do?" Jett asked. "Any ideas?"

Serious expression on his usually smiling face, Carlos paced as he processed the problem. "Ms. Diaz said she'll handle it. We *are* just kids, just students who can't even drive. Maybe Ruby is right and Sam's just living her life—the one outside of school." He threw up his hands in frustration. "I think we should try a little bit, but maybe give her space and let the grown-ups do their thing. Sí? They'll find her and tell us what we need to know." He gestured at Jett. "It's like when Jett was gone. I was so worried! And still, they only told me not to worry and that you'd be back. I *still* don't know where you went, but I know the teachers do and you didn't get into trouble for it, so it must have been okay." He was warming to the idea that there was nothing to worry about. "Yeah. This will be like that. *Just* like that. And it will be okay."

Ruby took a step towards him, put a hand on his arm, and smiled up at him.

Jett considered Carlos' hypothesis. "Just like that…" So Sam could be at the Learning Lodge? She would have to check with Dr. W to see if he knew anything. Quickly, she put a note into her phone to ask Dr. W later and then returned her focus to their conversation.

Andy's frown deepened. "I'm with Jett on this," he said. "I know we can't let it interfere with our school work and our own futures, but we need to find Sam. We need to know she's okay. And let's be practical here—we need to know if she's still part of our team. If she isn't, we need to adjust for that. What if she doesn't come back?"

Jett had never considered Sam *gone* gone, as in permanently and without a goodbye. She couldn't. She *wouldn't*.

"Sam is still part of our team and she *will* come back," she replied adamantly. "She's gone without telling anyone and that means we need to find her, maybe even to help her. She belongs with us, guys. I know, if the situation were reversed, she'd be the first one to look out for us. Am I right? Seriously. Who asked about me first when I went away?" Carlos nodded and looked persuaded. "That's what I thought. It was Sam, wasn't it? Well, we need to find her now. Are you in?"

Jett pinned each with her eyes until they answered. Everyone nodded, even Ruby, albeit more slowly than the boys. When that happened, she asked what she really wanted to know. "Who knows how?"

Everyone took a breath. Time to sort out how and who could do what. Jett's phone beeped with an alarm, intruding on the moment. She looked down at it. "Guys, I've got to go. We didn't get anywhere on our project, but we *did* figure out *something*. Something big. Sam is missing, and it's up to us to find her."

7

WITH NO DISCERNABLE progress on the case of her missing best friend, Jett's weekend had slowly meandered toward Monday, like a sloth on holiday. Finally! The academic week started again and she was glad to be back on campus. Her thoughts swirled as she paced around the parade grounds. She often thought of them as Carlos' athletic field. She wanted to focus, to be fully grounded in the present. Maybe she should reach down and touch the grass—note its temperature as well as texture. She had to—

"Hey! Watch out!"

A soccer ball flew at her, narrowly missing her face. Jett looked up to see a few members of the soccer team practicing their skills. One boy, who seemed vaguely familiar, waved. She lifted a hand. Now, where was she? Where was Carlos? Would he join his teammates soon? Looking around, she cataloged the time by what she saw and where she was. Yay! School. The parade grounds outside the main classroom building. Now, back to grounding. If only she could focus, if only she knew how to be here now and find the princess, who was first on her list for clarification on their project. Ruby *was* lead, after all. Jett stared out towards the Golden Gate Bridge. Arms folded squarely in front of her, she pursed her lips in concentration. Ah. There she was.

Out on the dew-covered grass, hands on hips and speaking with authority, Ruby stood in the quad, surrounded by her den of vipers. Déjà vu pestered Jett. She really needed to speak with Ruby right now, but she also wanted to avoid a repeat of the last time she encountered the nasty sycophants slithering all around the princess. Jett decided to text first and quickly fired off a single line: *We need to talk.*

Maybe Ruby would break away. Maybe Ruby would come to *her*. Oh, wait. In one of her mom's relationship books, she read that this would be considered a power play. Ruby would be conceding power to Jett if she sought her out. Or would she? Hmmm, Jett would have to reread that one and think about real-life applications. Meanwhile, she looked down at her phone. Waiting. No response, no text and not even a glance in her direction or a shrug of the shoulders. What should she do? Was it time to interrupt or wait for Ruby to see her first? Jett stomped her foot. Also a Ruby move, she realized, stomping her foot like an impatient child. She grinned to herself. Well, if the shoe fit…

Jett decided to go for it.

"Hey! Ruby!" She waited for Ruby to look her way. "Yeah. It's me. I mean, I know we're not friends outside of Foundations, but I thought you might like to take a break from…" Jett waved her arm around at Ruby's snake pit. "From *that*, and continue our conversation. We *do* have a problem or two to solve." She hoped this would entice Ruby. Jett didn't want to get any closer to that toxic tribe. She had learned her lesson last year when they practically drove her into the ground and then laughed as she fell. And no one came to help—not even Ruby. Jett had learned *that* lesson. No need for a repeat.

Through slitted eyes, Ruby studied her for a moment. "Oh. Hey, Jett. I don't know what you're on about, but my crew here knows everything anyway, so…" She shrugged before commanding: "Spill. Tell us all whatever it is and then just go." Ruby's eyebrows shot up as her speech slowed. She acted as if she were instructing someone simple. "Okay? You got that?" Rolling her eyes, she turned back to her friends.

Jett swallowed down the sour taste coating the insides of her cheeks. She squinted, too, watching the onlookers revel in nastiness. Jett wished Ruby knew her impact, how she led and how they followed. They practically worshipped her. Was it only last year that she had mistakenly believed Ruby was a victim and not the head viper?

Jett sighed. Here goes. "Well, two things. One: the project. And two: Sam. Which would you like to broadcast about first? I thought we were supposed to respect the group's privacy for both, but apparently that isn't your style. Did you want to talk about our project? Here? In front of everyone?" Heads turned and eyebrows raised. Smiles vanished and some seemed to hold their breath, proving Jett had once again caught them off guard.

"Actually, I'd like to start with Sam," Ruby retorted. "I'm on it. Did you know I already blasted all my feeds? I went live, *on camera*, talking about her, just this morning. We should hear back with results soon, and I imagine the ratings are off the charts!" She turned to the three worshipful snakes nearest to her. "You should totally check the numbers. I'm sure it went viral. I mean, did you see the tears I cried?" Ruby mocked a quivering lip and blinking back tears before breaking into a big grin. She angled her face toward the sky and opened her arms wide, pride painting every gesture and sound. "Such a brilliant post!"

Her phone started ringing a special ringtone. To Jett, it sounded like that song "Stronger" by Kelly Clarkson. Well, *that* was interesting.

"Ha! I was right! Here's my manager now. Just a sec." Ruby flapped a hand in the air, dismissing everyone, as she put the phone to her ear and turned her back on the crowd. Still, with bated breath, they all watched and waited .

"Hello, DeeDee. Um, yes. I did. No. I wasn't joking. No—No, I didn't. Um…" Ruby looked around. "No. No, I…" She looked down and her brows drew together before abruptly rising in surprise. "What? Wait, *what*?" Clutching the phone even tighter, her knuckles turned white. "You're telling me this *now*? Are you *kidding* me? *Seriously*? This is the first I'm hearing about it and you *do* mean *me*, right? Am I *not* your only client?"

Through clenched teeth, Ruby enunciated every syllable. "Get—Here—*Now*." She hung up and turned around. Then she turned around again. Ruby pivoted in a full circle a third time. She looked lost. Walking away as her crew started speaking, Ruby held up a hand to silence them, delivering a death look. No one followed.

She made a beeline for Jett. "Come on. We need to talk."

As they walked away together, Jett observed Ruby in her peripheral vision and waited for—something. After they had walked far enough away from the others, Ruby started to cry. Jett did not know what to do with that. Ruby crying? Huh. In front of her? Double huh.

Jett continued to wait as Ruby cried real tears. Unclear on how to be there for her, Jett fidgeted. She wasn't *Ruby's* best friend. Was Ruby the princess right now or just part of her Core5? Which role was she playing?

"I, um. I, uh, I screwed up. I can't—" Mascara blackened circles around her eyes and ran in splotchy lines down her cheeks. Ruby looked down at her shoes and back up at Jett. "I just can't handle this." With a quick glance back to make sure none of her posse had followed, Ruby swiped at her cheeks and collapsed onto a nearby bench. After a moment, Jett joined her.

Jett tilted her head, still stumped as to how she was meant to respond. She didn't know what to say. Is *that* what you say when you don't know what to say and someone else is being honest with you? Jett thought she might try it. "Ruby, I don't know what to say."

For a long, silent moment, Ruby searched her face. Jett could see the heartbreak. "Of course you don't. You would have never gotten yourself into this situation. How could you?"

Jett thought to herself: what situation?

A slick little smart car pulled up to them. When a twenty-something woman dressed in the latest ready-for-anything-but-still-cooler-than-you uniform of overpriced, cause-supporting sneakers and thick-framed glasses jumped out and came running over, Jett instinctively took a small step back. The stranger ignored Jett completely. A self-congratulatory mix of confidence and relief washed over the newcomer's features before she schooled them into concern.

"Ruby, oh, Ru! I didn't know. Your parents are going to fire me. I thought you knew!" She wrung her hands despondently. A riot of colorfully beaded wristbands peeked from under her shirtsleeve. "I thought they had had *the* talk with you about it all and how to be safe. Well—safer, I guess. That's why I've been scripting all of your feeds."

She paused and then seemed to go on the defensive. "Didn't you know? Didn't you wonder? It was all to keep you safe. The police think they have a lead and he isn't local, but your dad isn't so sure. He wants us to go dark. He's been pushing for it for a while—but now with the live you did this morning?" She threw her hands up in resignation. "You didn't run it by anyone! Now people are wondering about this Sam person and you've got to close that loop. We need a Sam on your feed or we can't go dark. You're in danger and now we can't stop posting."

Her voice rose as her desperation grew. "But each post could put you in further danger. Your dad is freaked. We need to *leave. NOW.*"

Exasperated, Jett interrupted.

"I'm sorry, but you're making my friend upset and I don't know what you're talking about. What feed? What's a live? How is Sam involved? Try again. Explain it to me like I don't know what you mean. Because I don't."

Startled, DeeDee looked at Jett as if she had just magically appeared out of thin air. She glanced at Ruby, who nodded, but with more contrition than Jett had ever seen before. What was going on?

Glossy locks, the color of freshly brewed coffee, bounced with every micro movement and touch of the salty bay breeze as DeeDee's head swiveled back and forth. Her confused gaze ricocheted between them. "I'm sorry. I don't know you," she said, finally fixing a glare on Jett. "Have we met? Somewhere important? An event, maybe? I don't think so. I remember *everybody.* Who *are* you?"

"I'm Jett Harper. And Ruby came to *me*, so I think you need to tell me what's going on if you want my help." She paused for a moment as recognition dawned. Although she had asked, DeeDee *didn't* want to know who she was. This DeeDee woman was laughing at her. How rude! "You *do* want me to help, right?" She looked at Ruby, who was nodding at her. Jett returned her attention to DeeDee. "Ruby wants me to help, so I will. Please, I'm asking again—nicely even. Please explain it to me. From the beginning."

DeeDee's laughter had an edge of hysteria to it, but she got it under control. "Okay, Jett Harper," she said, taking a deep breath. "I don't know you, but I guess Ruby can vouch for you. Here's the deal." She stopped again, looking to Ruby one more time.

"Oh, for heaven's sake!" Ruby erupted. "I'll tell her what I know, then you can fill us both in."

"Jett, you've heard of social media, right? Facebook, YouTube, Instagram, TikTok—that kind of thing? Well, I'm kind of—kind of a big deal there."

Yes, Jett had known that for more than a year. She nodded encouragingly at Ruby. "You mean a Breakfast Club-style Princess, right?"

"Yeah, you got me to watch that old movie," Ruby acknowledged. "My parents were over the moon about that. I guess I *am* kind of like that Claire character, but here's the thing. I'm *also* different. I have a mission, something to *do*. I'm the real deal. I don't *just* look pretty. I bring joy and information on what's good. I influence my followers *for* the good. And so, I have a lot of followers." She looked at DeeDee. "DeeDee is my…"

DeeDee watched with keen interest. Head tilted, she didn't interrupt. Ruby huffed and rolled her eyes.

"She's my social media manager. She makes sure only the best content makes it out into the world." Ruby looked down for a moment, struggling to keep herself under control, before continuing. "But this morning, I was bored. It ticked me off that everything has to go through DeeDee, like I don't know what to say to my own followers. And it upset me that everything about our project is on hold until we find Sam. I mean, it's finally my turn to be in charge at school and she takes *my* spotlight?"

Ruby ran her fingers through her hair, pulling in frustration. "So I went rogue. I made a live video without script or clearance. I posted about Sam going missing so we could find her." She looked at her phone. "See? It's already gotten like 6.4 million views." Ruby smiled, but DeeDee frowned and jumped in.

"I'm trying to take it down, but it's trending and I can't get the sites to cooperate."

Jett tilted her head in tandem with Ruby. DeeDee's voice grew louder.

"The *problem* is that Ruby exposed where she goes

to school, where she is, and where Sam might be. Ruby has stalkers—at least five that we're tracking—and now these random weirdos, who I can almost guarantee are watching this over and over, they can hunt for Sam, and *might*, maybe, but they can also find Ruby. And they will. You're *all* exposed. And it isn't safe."

As if to emphasize the point, a phone chimed in with a hypnotic tune. DeeDee glanced at it and went pale. "Oh no! It's your father," she hissed nervously at Ruby before answering the call.

"Hello, Mr. Stefano. Yes. Yes, sir. Actually, I'm with her right now." She locked eyes with Ruby and grimaced. "Okay. Yes. I will. I can do that. We're on our way."

"Okay, Dee, spill," Ruby said, looking resigned.

"Well, Ru, your dad says you're under lockdown. No more anything for you for a while—like, until this blows over and you're safe." She tucked her phone into a tiny pocket purse attached to her hip and took Ruby by the elbow. "You can connect with your team for schoolwork, but you're going away—into hiding. I'm to bring you to him now."

Ruby wrenched her arm out of DeeDee's grasp. "*What?* Wait a minute! He can't do that! He can't just shut me down. I've done nothing wrong! I've only tried to help find a classmate who isn't answering her phone!" She backed away as DeeDee advanced on her. "And neither one of you told me anything about any stalkers. So, no! Just no. You can't just take me. I refuse!"

Jett felt bad for Ruby, but was at a complete loss about how to help her.

DeeDee looked grim as she made another grab for Ruby's arm. "Actually, I can. I've full permission and he said if you don't come with me, you won't like the consequences. I don't know what that means exactly, but he says you do." She changed tactics as Ruby sidestepped her grasp again, holding both hands up placatingly. "Please, Ruby. Please, Ruru, just come with me so we can get through this."

Ruby had blanched at DeeDee's mention of consequences. Her anger subsided quickly and she turned toward Jett with a chastened air. "Looks like I'm going to be gone for now, too. But at least you know what's happening with me." She put out a hand. "Give me your phone for a minute. I'll put myself in so you can text me." She studied Jett for a long moment. "You will, won't you? This time around you'll text me, too? Like you do the rest of our Core5?"

Jett nodded mutely. She would text Ruby. She needed to text the boys, too. There was a lot to explain.

As Ruby turned to hand herself over to DeeDee, she thought of one more thing. "Hey, Jett? Avoid the vipers. You were right last year. They are nasty and they spit venom," she said, looking apologetic. "I don't want you to get caught up in their stuff, okay? Just stick to the boys. I'll be back as soon as I can." And with that, she left.

Jett stood by helplessly and watched her go. This was a first; she never thought she would miss Ruby, but here they were. The Core5 had two team members gone, both possibly in trouble. Jett had to sort out who to help first and what to do. The first part was easy: Sam. She had to find Sam. Then she would find Ruby. The boys would help figure out the next steps. Jett texted them one word.

> HELP.

8

SEVERAL HOURS LATER, Jett collapsed onto her bed at home. The boys had both responded, but Carlos was busy with his responsibilities as captain for the soccer team and Andy had family commitments. They hadn't asked what was wrong and she hadn't said. So it was all up to Jett. Again. She couldn't believe the number of complications filling her life. They overwhelmed her. She needed to sort through all that she knew and set up some kind of plan. Deciding to work in her room, away from her mother's prying eyes, she created three boards—one for Ruby and her stalkers, one for Sam and her silence, and one for Yoda-Gus and his task list. She was so tired. Fuel. She needed fuel. Jett wandered down to the kitchen.

"Hey, kiddo! How's your day?" asked Daddio.

Although she was glad to see him, Jett couldn't muster so much as a smile. Instead, she shrugged. Body shutting down, she noted that her brain currently traversed the winding paths of thought that Daddio called a rabbit hole. She felt the weight of his scrutiny tugging her back from the edge of that hole and realized she headed that way more and more often lately. She should put a note about that on the dog board, Jett thought listlessly. But that was back in her room. Right now, she saw only one option to avoid falling into the abyss.

"That looks good," she said. "Will you please make me a sandwich?"

Mouth open for his first bite, Daddio smiled, put the sandwich back on its plate, and handed it over. Good timing, she thought. He started making another. When he finished, they sat down together and ate.

"I have a question." She paused a moment. "Actually, I have way more than one, but I'll start there. When you thought a dog could help me and you talked to the people about it, how did you get them to agree?" Jett swallowed hard, unsure she wanted the answer to her follow-up question. She asked anyway. "What did you say?"

Daddio scrutinized the sandwich in his hands for a moment before he responded. "Well, Bug, I just told them about the whole disappearing thing, and then you going silent, and then about the Learning Lodge. I told them what I saw with Gus."

He put down the sandwich and looked into her eyes, gauging her reaction. Leaning forward, he ensured he would catch her every expression as he continued.

"They asked me to send them some medical records, so I did," he said gently. "I included the reports from the Lodge and they said you're a great fit for one of their dogs. I asked them how. They said it's pretty individual, but gave me some examples. Then they offered to put you on the waitlist, but they warned me it's very long."

He brightened slightly and smiled at her. "That could be a good thing, though, because it gives us time to observe where you might need help. Eventually, you'll be paired with a dog and that's when they would help us sort out what tasks would help you the most. Then your dog would finish training by learning how to help you specifically."

Jett sat back and pondered. Right now, she wanted a dog who could sniff out danger, a dog who could find Sam. She knew that wasn't what he meant, but wouldn't it be cool if she had one of those? Suddenly, she had a thought. "Do they also train those search-and-rescue dogs?"

He shook his head. "I don't think so, Sweets. They pretty much focus on dogs that can help individuals with daily tasks." He chuckled as he picked up his sandwich again. "Why? Do you need a search-and-rescue dog for something?" He took a bite, still chortling. But Jett wasn't laughing.

She took a deep breath. This was a moment of truth. How much could she tell him? What would he keep private? She reached into her pocket and pulled out some change. She handed it to him and he took it without thinking. "Attorney-client privilege, Daddio."

He raised an eyebrow and swallowed the bite he'd been chewing. "Wait. What? Why?" His hand tightened around the change he was holding as he looked into her troubled face.

"I don't want you to talk about this with Mom or anyone, really, without us deciding together, okay? These are my secrets, and I need you to keep them for me," she said. "Some of them aren't *even* my secrets. And if I'm going to tell anyone else's secrets, I need to keep track of exactly who knows them, too. Does that make sense? I'm invoking attorney-client privilege." She bit into her own sandwich and waited for him to respond.

"Um, okay, Jett. You got it. Now, as your attorney and not just your dad, I'm telling you to spill. Tell me everything."

And so she did. She told him about last summer, when she spent most of her time deep in research about how to be a best friend to Sam. And that was the problem. How could she be a best friend if Sam was a ghost?

Filling in the gaps, she told him about Sam's music and about how she had figured out that Sam was poor. She told him about Sam singing on the public transport system, in the stations and on the street, just so she could eat and get to school. She shared that Sam was teaching her to sing, that Sam lived with her Grams and her sister, but that Miya left with the *Hamilton* touring cast and ever since then Sam had been acting weird. Jett told him what Miya had said about them living in a one-bedroom apartment, all three of them. She talked about Sam not answering texts or showing up anymore and she told him how she had promised Miya she would be Sam's best friend and not give up. The story poured out of her—all her worry, all her confusion and that despite many hours spent trying to sort the right next action, she didn't know what to do. Finally, she swore him to secrecy again. No one else knew any of this, she explained, because she had promised Sam she wouldn't expose her secrets. Jett wanted to be the *best* best friend ever and even now that she understood she wouldn't be—after all, she was violating the code by telling these secrets—it was okay. Finding Sam was more important than any label.

Daddio just stared at her. He opened his mouth like he was going to speak and then shut it again. He opened his mouth. Then shut it. Jett laughed. He looked like he was mimicking their neighbor Ben's fish impression. Jett wondered at what age boys turned into men who acted like fish, breathing through their mouths underwater.

Shaking himself out of his silence, Daddio asked, "What's so funny, kiddo?"

Jett tried to stifle her laughter, but couldn't quite manage it. She said nothing more.

"You just told me a lot I didn't know, but I didn't think any of it was funny. Did I miss something?"

Jett laughed again and felt relieved to be laughing. She couldn't help it. He thought *that* was a lot? Wait until he learned about Princess Ruby and her being imprisoned in a secret tower! Jett thought maybe Sam and Ruby needed assistance dogs too.

"Oh, Daddio. Seriously? That's just part of what I have to tell you!" she said, shaking her head at the overwhelming chaos of it all. "It's the most urgent part to me, but still—there's more!"

Sitting back in his chair as if she'd pushed him there, he blinked. "There's *more*? Kiddo, you better tell me now before I start pacing. This already is pretty big stuff." Daddio looked anxious. Didn't he have a lawyer game face or something? Strangely enough, his anxiety reassured her she wasn't blowing things out of proportion. Clearly, she needed to let him in on the rest.

"Remember Ruby, that influencer girl Mom is so impressed with? Apparently, she got into trouble with her dad and some assistant named DeeDee might get fired because Ruby went on her own social media feed and posted about Sam being missing," she said, speaking slowly as she thought things through while she talked. "Ruby really doesn't know very much, other than that Sam is missing, but she *did* tell the entire world which school they both attend. This freaked out Ruby's dad because Ruby has stalkers and now they know exactly where to look for her. He's worried about one stalker in particular, so Ruby's been whisked away to some secret location. She didn't even know about the stalkers, though!"

Feeling a brief moment of anger at the injustice of it, Jett relived the moment when Ruby got in the car and left. Then she realized she hadn't told Daddio the most important part. "Ruby was in charge of our Foundations project for the year. So now what do we do? Sam's gone and Ruby's gone, so now we're down to a Core3 instead of a Core5!"

There was that feeling of injustice again. Was this typical? Schoolwork and grades may have dropped a bit on her list of priorities as she'd been learning how to relate to people, but they still formed a critical framework around her life.

Taking a couple deep breaths, she tried to manage her growing frustration. Daddio studied her quietly. "She texted me she doesn't want to do the same topic anyway, because it feels unsafe with everything going on. Now, with only three of us left to work on the project, how are we supposed to find a new topic and start all over? And what about Sam? We need to find her. I don't know where to begin, or what to do, or which problem to tackle first. Then there's this whole question of a dog. I mean, really, how could one help me with any of this? It sounds to me like my friends need help, too, maybe more than me. A search-and-rescue dog could find Sam. Maybe a guard dog could protect Ruby?"

At last, she fell silent and waited to see what Daddio would say or do. She wanted her boards. She wanted data. Most of all, she was worried. She had no action plan.

Daddio pinched the bridge of his nose and sighed deeply. Then he stood up from the table, trailing sandwich crumbs as he began to pace. "Huh. Wow. Okay," he said softly after his first circuit of the room. Pacing was his usual way of thinking things through. Jett watched him clasp his hands behind his back, bow his head, and wander around the room, lost in thought. Daddio summarized what he'd just heard. "Ruby Stefano has stalkers. Sam is a poor, missing black girl that no one seems to know how to find. And you don't see any difference between your needs and theirs." He nodded as he paced. "Three separate problems. Three separate solutions." He stopped pacing and gave her a determined, grim look. "Where do you want to start?"

"Sam. Sam is what's bothering me the most," she told him without a moment's hesitation. "How do I keep my promise to Miya when I don't know where Sam is? I need your help. Don't *you* know what to do about this? If you don't, I don't know who does." Jett could feel tears welling in her eyes. She couldn't look at him. She wanted to finish before her emotions leaked out of her eyes. "I've been breaking my brain trying to sort it out, and the best solution I've come up with is a search-and-rescue dog. But I don't even have anything of hers for a dog to smell so they can find her! I'm worried. Really, really worried."

At this, she started to cry. This embarrassed her, but she didn't have a choice. She was already pulling at her neck and jogging her right leg up and down. She didn't know what else she could do to get rid of all the emotions flooding her system.

Daddio rushed to her and put his arms around her shoulders, squeezing her tight, just as she liked. Jett turned into him and put her arms around his middle, pressing the tears into his shirt. They clung to each other for a moment, each lost in their own worlds.

"Bug-a-boo—do you know what my worst fear is?" he asked softly, still holding her. "It would be losing you. I just can't even imagine. Our firm started working with local law enforcement on a task team for missing children last year. I just had to after that one moment of you being gone, and that was only for a few hours. How are you holding up with your friend gone for so long now? Didn't you tell me she has no parents, just her Grams? Do you even know what town she lives in or what part of the Bay Area? You said she takes the BART train and then some buses. I imagine the bus you're talking about is the PresidiGo shuttle. Does she take BART from the East Bay then? "

Jett nodded, pulling back to look up at his face, but not letting go. "I think she lives in Oakland or something."

He smoothed her hair with his hand affectionately. "Okay. I don't know anyone over there on our team, but I'm sure someone does. Do you have a picture of her?"

Jett pulled out her phone. She had only one photo on it, the one of her Core5 after winning the Freshman Faire. She showed it to him. "This is all I have."

He took her phone and zoomed in on Sam. "Mind if I send this to myself? I need to share it with people who can help. Can I assume you've spoken about this with your teachers? Doctor Williams, maybe, or the administration?"

Jett shook her head, and his eyebrows lifted in response.

"But Daddio, wait a minute. It was one thing for me to tell you Sam's secrets, but now more people will know, and she'll know I told them. Do we really have to? Can't we just, you know, keep it between us?"

He loosened his grip on her, but kept his eyes locked on hers, his hands on her shoulders. "We could keep it between us," he said doubtfully, "but hasn't Ruby already told the world that Sam's missing? What we need to focus on right now is finding her. Tell me everything you can think of and we can do that. Did you say she sings on the street to pay for things? And she's teaching you to sing? Does she have other students? Maybe that's a way we can find her."

Jett almost started to cry again. She looked down into her lap, thinking.

"No, she doesn't. She only taught me a few times. And yes, that's where my 'mad money', as Mom calls it, went," she said. "But the last time she gave it back and said she didn't want my money. She told me she might be gone for a while. Do you think she knew this was going to happen? That she would leave and not come back and just not tell me?" That thought really hurt.

Daddio gave her another squeeze before sitting down next to her. "No, Jett. No," he said emphatically. "I think when life happens, sometimes we can't predict what will happen next—especially when we change up our patterns. Sam probably didn't expect to be gone this long, but you said she wasn't responding on her phone. That's what worries me most. I mean, don't all kids use their phones all the time? I'm not really sure how to find a kid that isn't on social media and isn't answering their phone."

Determined to exude confidence, he went back to square one. "The school will at least know where she lives. Maybe we should start there," he said. "Want me to speak with someone officially, as a member of the missing kids' team, or as your solicitor? Even though good ol' Daddio is my favorite title, I don't think it's enough for them because I'm not *her* Daddio. Speaking of, do you know what happened there? You said her Grams is raising her. What's the deal with her parents?"

Jett shrugged, frustrated that she couldn't tell him much more. "Yeah, her Grams and her sister. But her sister is gone for now, so now it's just her Grams," she said. "Sam once told me it's been just her and her sister for as long as she could remember, so I don't think her parents were ever around much. And her Grams used to work, like, three jobs, but she's getting too old. So now she has one job and Sam and her sister try to pick up the slack. How do people work three jobs? I just don't understand how that's possible."

Daddio reached out and squeezed her hand sympathetically. "Baby girl, I don't either. When I went to university, I worked and went to school during my undergrad, but it was brutal. It certainly spurred me on to do what I had to so that I wouldn't ever have to have more than one job at a time again. Do you know her Grams' name?"

Jett just shook her head, feeling the tears welling up again. "I don't know much, do I?" she choked out. She stopped and cleared her throat. "Am I really so bad at this friend thing? Shouldn't I have asked her at some point? I think I need to ask more questions. But it's not like I don't want to know. I'm just trying to respect privacy. I don't understand how to find the balance. What can you ask and what do you let people keep to themselves? No wonder I failed."

She shifted unhappily in her seat, aching for answers and tempted to wallow in the overwhelm of it all. But—no. That wasn't an option. Her friends needed help. She squared her shoulders and got back down to business. "Now let's talk about Ruby," she said. I mean, *stalkers*? It's like in the movies, but this is real life! Did you know that was even a real thing? I thought it was just something on TV, like zombies and werewolves, but scarier. Ruby gave me her number so I would text with her. Does that mean we're friends now and, if we are, are we everywhere friends or only friends in class? I can text her about our projects without making her come to campus, I guess.

Is that how it works? How do I keep it straight? Maybe I should ask her. She'll know. Sam says if you have to ask if you can, the answer is you can't, but maybe she's wrong. Is she wrong?"

Daddio, struggling to keep up with her, put up his hands in mock surrender. "Whoa! So complex! I didn't realize that kind of thing still existed with you kids today, but I guess it makes sense." He ran his fingers through his hair, thinking. "Okay, kiddo, let's talk in generalities before specifics. Let's get some definitions out of the way, so we're on the same page, okay?"

"Okay," Jett said, glad to see him digging in again.

"Here's what I know: You have friends, and then you have associates, and you also have acquaintances," he ticked off the three categories on his fingers. "Sometimes they're a progression," he said, pointing rapidly between his three extended fingers, "like from acquaintance to associate if you have a joint interest or project or something, or from acquaintance to friend if you have a fondness for each other as well as common interests. Is this making sense?"

Jett nodded, furrowing her brow and paying close attention as he continued.

"There is really only one kind of friend," he said. "Yes, there are certain qualifiers to that. There are different levels of friendship, like you've been studying. There are best friends and casual friends, but even casual friends don't have limits on the 'where.' If someone puts limits on where they'll be friendly, that sounds more like an acquaintance. Seriously. People don't even count as friends until you can speak to each other or spend time together, no matter where you are. That's a friend. Anything else isn't good enough."

That made sense, Jett thought. It filled in a missing piece of her friend's puzzle. But did that mean acquaintances aren't a priority? Daddio should be able to clarify that.

"Does that mean friends are more important?" she asked. "That they matter most?"

"Again, that depends. Now we're talking priorities, aren't we?" he stopped and gave her a time-out sign, bouncing his right palm against his extended left fingers. "Seriously, we could spend all day on this. Why don't we get back to sorting the problems at hand, and then see where we are?"

Her head was swirling with ideas and a growing hope that she could find a way through all this. But she knew that she had picked Daddio's brain enough for one afternoon. It was time to do something more concrete than just talk.

"Daddio, can we make boards? I started to. I'm going to keep them in my room, but I need to see something to study each of these issues."

"That's a great idea," he said, smiling broadly at her.

Jett ran off to continue what she had started.

> Sam
> 1) no phone 2) probably in oakland 3) with Grams 4) or at Bart station 5) look for her

> Ruby
> 1) hiding from stalkers 2) could text now 3) tell boys 4) change group project 5) but to what?

Maybe there was a project that would leverage something they were already doing. At this late date, it was important not to add too much to their workload. Could they do a project around finding Sam? Or maybe they could do something on Ruby and stalkers. Or maybe even helper dogs. Seriously, what did each of these things have in common?

As she waited for the answer to magically appear, Jett could feel her lips puckering, eyes squinting, and brain sputtering. Hmmm. Oh. Yeah. Okay—what about safety? Would the boys find *that* interesting? It seemed to be important for Sam and Ruby, but would it matter, really, to her and the boys? Was safety something they could work on for an *entire* school year? Maybe—if you considered that they *did* have to find their friend, defeat a group of stalkers, and keep Jett from going silent, or passing out, or melting down. Yeah, safety might be *exactly* what they needed to focus on. She would talk to the boys tomorrow. Decision made, it surprised her when her stomach grumbled at her. Her sandwich! She had forgotten all about it.

Bouncing back down the stairs, she felt worlds better. Jett stopped as she entered the kitchen and studied her Daddio, who looked like he had aged five years since she had asked him for that sandwich. Poor Daddio. He was getting older by the day and her problems sure weren't helping. Pretty soon, she would have to learn to make him sandwiches just the way he liked, too. Jett made a mental note. Pay attention. Make better sandwiches. But first, she would eat the one waiting in front of her.

9

TIME PASSED TOO quickly and yet somehow altogether too slowly. Even being back in the classroom didn't dispel the tension she carried in her throat and shoulders. It choked joy and leached all color from her life. Jett struggled to stay present. With overwhelm hitting her hard, she just couldn't address all the intense situations affecting her. Sam. Sam was her focus, but Jett still had no idea where she was.

Yesterday, Ms. Diaz had told what was left of her Core5 that Sam wasn't answering her phone and neither was her guardian. She had apologized for not recognizing Sam wasn't living with two parents, but just a grandmother. Just? Wasn't Sam's grandmother the responsible type? Grandmothers were older than parents. By default, wouldn't she know more and be able to take *better* care of Sam? From the bits of information she had, Jett concluded Grams was super-reliable. Knowing Grams also wasn't answering her phone ratcheted Jett's anxiety and newly labeled depression to entirely new levels. This sluggish, oozing, morose molasses infiltrating her system—the one that overpowered the agitated sharpness of anxiety—presented as a textbook case of depression. Jett knew because she had looked it up. Was there any hope? There had to be. She needed there to be. Today she would get answers. She was here in class before every other student for just this purpose, and Ms. Diaz, thank goodness, was early, too.

The moment Ms. Diaz crossed the threshold into the classroom, Jett pounced. "Can you please share Sam's address with me? I want to check on her."

Ms. Diaz gave her a sympathetic look but shook her head. "Sorry but—no. I don't have it to give to you and I couldn't even if I did. That's not my call to make."

Jett was stunned. "What? You don't have it? Why not? Surely the administration does. Won't they share it with you?" She wished she had gotten Miya's number that night after *Hamilton*. Miya would have told her what was going on.

Ms. Diaz walked to a student desk and sat down, gesturing to Jett to sit across from her. "Look, I know you're worried and that this isn't what you want to hear," she said. "But I've done all I can do—all that I'm *allowed* to do. I've told the principal and her team about the situation. They'll take it from here. Please don't worry. They can handle this. They did while you were gone last year, right? This is the same thing, really."

To Jett, it was *not* the same thing, not the same thing at all! She knew where she was. She didn't know where Sam was. How was that the same? Her thoughts were spinning and she didn't like where they were taking her.

Trying hard not to spiral inside of herself, she realized that Ms. Diaz was still speaking. "In the meantime, your team is now down two students. That's 40% of your team. Also, from what I understand, Ruby was lead on this year's project. So have you and the boys discussed what you'll do now and who will keep you on track? Are you thinking you'll pursue the same topic or are you going to pivot and rethink the project? Of course, I'll grant you more time because of extenuating circumstances, but you need to have a new hypothesis to me in the next few days. Okay?"

Jett was stuck on the concept of "Ruby being lead" meaning she kept them on track. Is that what Ms. Diaz believed? Is that what a lead usually did? Because, if so, Ruby wasn't the lead—or if she was, she had failed miserably at it. If keeping the team on track was the primary definition of being lead, then that role fell to Andy. Well, that was unexpected—but also oddly reassuring. Maybe they hadn't lost so much after all.

Jett refocused on Ms. Diaz and discovered that the teacher was watching her, waiting for her to respond in some way. Jett didn't know what the teacher was expecting, so she simply nodded and started texting what was left of the team. What else could she do?

Another topic encroached on her myopic focus. Should she text Ruby now and let her know that she'd both defined and executed wrong on being a lead? Maybe she *should* get her buy-in on changing the project focus, but she didn't have time for Ruby's drama and she didn't want to be derailed from what needed to be done. She didn't need to text Ruby right away. On the other hand, she did need to text Carlos and Andy. It was up to the boys and her to decide what to do next. The three of them were all that was left of the team.

"Guys, Ms. Diaz says we have a few days to confirm or change our team's hypothesis. Are we changing up our project? We need to discuss."

Carlos sent back a thumbs up. With lightning speed, Andy shot back: *"When. Now? Can we meet up now? I'm in the cafe."*

She took a deep breath and gave Ms. Diaz a firm nod. "I'm going to meet with what's left of my Core5 now. Thank you for your update, Ms. Diaz, although, to be honest, I don't think it's good enough."

Disconcerted, Ms. Diaz rocked back in her chair as Jett hoisted her backpack and walked out.

JETT PEERED THROUGH the multi-paned windows of the Campus Cafe that overlooked a magnificent view across the San Francisco Bay. As she strolled up the meandering, manicured path that led away from the Golden Gate Bridge, she marveled again at the beauty of their school's landscape. The wind whipping off the bay sighed through the eucalyptus trees around her as birds chirped and flitted between their branches and a fog horn resonated underneath it all. Salty air mixed with the aroma of coffee and cakes as she opened the door. Every time she moved around the campus, her body relaxed more, as if it knew this was her place. How she loved it here.

Inside, a crowd of kids surrounded Andy. They all had the same skin tone that Jett had come to associate with his Indian heritage. She wondered if their families were all from Gujarat, the state that Andy and his family were from. Jett heard laughter and saw flashes of white teeth as they interacted happily; she wondered what it would be like to be part of such a tight-knit community. Maybe community *should* be their project focus. But Jett was still worried about Sam's safety, and now Ruby's as well, albeit in different ways.

"Hey, Andy, I don't mean to interrupt," she said, abruptly silencing the table full of students around him. "But I *do* have a question. I hope it doesn't come across as rude."

He smiled at her and quietly gestured that the others should give him the table. Most of the crowd moved off to other tables, but a couple of girls lingered nearby, eavesdropping. He stood and pulled out a chair for her. "Ask away," he said as Jett shed her Spiketus Rex and sat down. "Whatever it is, I promise to think about who is asking versus what words you use."

Good, Jett thought. That would do nicely. She took a moment to sort out what she wanted to say while they waited for Carlos to arrive. Her curiosity had been building for a while. Was it okay to ask? Might as well find out. She jumped in.

"Your friends all have the same beautiful skin and you're all speaking something besides English," she said, a bit nervous about how he might react. "I was just wondering: do you consider yourself just American or are you American, but something else first? I did some research and people from India are Indian by nationality but not by ethnicity or language, so it's confusing to me."

Andy sat down next to her and smiled warmly. "I actually don't spend a lot of time thinking about it. It's like I have a strong community of extended family more than anything else. I think I just consider myself American with a big, reliable family who have immigrated from India. Does that help?" He cocked his head to one side as if he'd just thought of something. "Dadi is still asking when you are coming over. She thinks you need to try her khichdi because I told her you haven't had it before and now she's worried. She wants to know what you eat and how you stay healthy." He smirked briefly, but it quickly turned into a fond smile. Jett felt some of the tension leave her body.

The girls listening in giggled. One of them, a beauty with thick dark hair flowing down past her shoulder blades, piped up. "I want to be there for that, when you bring her home."

A flush rose in his cheeks, but he kept his face firmly set in a warm smile. He wouldn't make eye contact with her, but Jett concluded he must be thinking of his grandmother. She didn't want to interrupt his train of thought, but they had things to work on.

"Okay. Thanks for explaining and I do still want to meet your family," she reassured him. "For now, though, we have problems. *Big* problems…"

Carlos came running in. He threw his soccer duffle into a chair, held up a hand, then turned and jogged to the counter to order food. He kept moving his legs up and down even though he was in front of the counter, studying the menu as if it held the secrets to the universe. Jett marveled at the ceaseless whirlwind that was Carlos. She smiled as his hands landed on the counter and he craned his neck to include them, legs still pumping. "Hey, Manita, Andy! Want anything?" he yelled across the room. "I'm starving!"

Andy smiled shyly at Jett and raised his eyebrows. When she said nothing, he took charge and answered for both of them. "Yeah, Jett needs a hot chocolate and one of those Rice Krispy things. I'm good though. I've been here a while."

"Perfecto! I love it! I'll be right over." Carlos turned around to order.

The pretty girls who had been eavesdropping took it all in, fascinated. Andy waved them away. "Sorry, guys, but we've got work to do on our super-secret sophomore project. See you later?" Long-Hair Girl smiled sweetly and winked at him before she stood and sashayed over to a new group of friends. Still waiting for Carlos to return, Jett watched them go and decided to risk asking one more thing. "Can I ask you another question?" Andy dipped his head once to encourage her.

"When you saw Sam on BART that one time, were you going to or from school? What was she doing?" Jett was really curious if he knew Sam's secret, but maybe Sam didn't know he knew about her singing for money on the trains.

Andy pondered for a moment, rubbing the back of his neck. "I think she was just sitting there looking out the window. I was with my friends, so I didn't pay too much attention, to be honest. The next thing I knew, she wasn't there. I mean, I *thought* I saw her, but I'm not sure. Maybe I just thought I did. Know what I mean?"

Jett knew exactly what he meant. She also knew Sam probably had been there, and then slipped out to another car where she could sing without him knowing. It sounded to her like Sam was successful. She had hidden her truth well. What would it be like to hide your truth—to have a public life you kept separate? And why would you do that? She had so many questions, some of which only Sam could answer. Jett suddenly felt lonely and made a mental note of this new sensation. Before she had friends, she never felt lonely. Now that she knew what having a best friend was like, she hated going without. Sam *had* to come back. Jett wanted to help Sam not worry about keeping her talents a secret anymore. Eyes filling with tears, she blinked rapidly to clear them. Oh, Sam. She missed her.

Carlos got back just in time. Jett almost spilled Sam's secret *again*, and that's not the type of friend she wanted to be; in fact, it wasn't the type of friend she wanted to have, either.

"Hey-hey! Here you go!" Carlos handed Jett the biggest Rice Krispies treat she had ever seen and a minty-smelling hot chocolate. "Don't freak out on me. I wanted to make it a surprise. I had them make a peppermint hot chocolate. You like peppermint, right, Manita? Everyone likes peppermint. Even those locos who don't like chocolate!"

Change always threw Jett for a loop. She wanted to be grateful, but, without any preamble, Carlos had just assumed she was ready for something new. How should she handle that? Jett looked at the cup and brought it to her nose. She sniffed hesitantly. It was different, but she didn't want to disappoint Carlos. She wanted to try it and she hoped fervently that she would like it. At the very least, Jett was grateful for his thoughtfulness! Would Carlos read her face and see gratitude even if she didn't like it? She hoped so. Jett took a tentative sip. Mmm. This was good!

She grinned, whipped cream on her upper lip. "Thank you, Carlos. This is delicious!"

Pleased with himself, Carlos grinned back at her. "Sí, Sí. I'm glad you like it, Manita!"

As she took another sip, he turned to Andy. "Do you know why we're here? I sent a text to Ruby but she said she wasn't coming. What's up with that? Isn't she supposed to be in charge? Not cool."

Surprised, Jett shifted her gaze between the two of them. Jett hadn't expected Andy to know Ruby was in hiding, but wouldn't Carlos already have known? Weren't they a couple? Jett felt her stomach clench at the thought that she might have to expose Ruby's secrets, too. What if that put her in even more danger? What was she supposed to say or not say? Did this mean she wouldn't be worthy of being Ruby's friend? The boys were looking at her expectantly. She tensed and began pulling on her neck.

Feeling the pressure build, she huffed and cleared her throat. She decided to deflect what she could. "Carlos, I thought you were on Ruby's social media! I forgot all the names of those places, but she *did* try to tell me the other day. Do you know how to watch what she puts on her channel or whatever? I was doing some research and—"

Carlos laughing baffled Jett. "Hold up, hold up! You mean to tell me you're not following Ruby—not even on *one* site? I thought everyone did! Come here, 'Nita. Andy, pull up something recent, yeah? Maybe the one about Sam?"

Andy pulled out his phone and fiddled with it for a bit. He pulled up the video as requested. Jett and Carlos leaned in as Andy pressed play.

Jett watched Ruby make a plea for help to find Sam. Ruby described her. She told the audience where she had last seen her—in class on the campus of Presidio Prep—and how Sam had just left with no trace of her since. She made it seem like Sam had been kidnapped or something! Ruby acted like finding Sam was important to her, like it should be important to everyone else. She pleaded. She cried and, it seemed to Jett, Ruby looked scared. When the video stopped, Jett swallowed. Hard.

"Did you see how many views? Seriously! That girl is a genius!" Carlos said excitedly. "It's everywhere now. Someone for sure will find Sam for us." Andy showed Jett where to look for how many people had watched. She read a few of the thousands of comments. Tears filled her eyes. She felt herself closing in and reached out for Carlos' hand to anchor herself.

"'Nita! What is it?" Carlos clung to her hand. Andy knelt down in front of her and caught her gaze. "Are you having a panic attack? My friend has those. We need to breathe when it happens. Want to breathe with me?" Jett nodded and Andy started counting as they practiced focused breathing. Carlos joined in with his over-the-top attempts. He made it clear that he was all in—even if he had no idea what he was doing. His ham-handed efforts brought Jett back from the brink. She couldn't both focus on her breathing and laugh at Carlos' antics, so she just gave up and laughed. Oh, Carlos!

It was clear to her now. She had to tell them what was going on—and soon, while she still could. She squeezed Carlos' hand one more time, patted it, gave Andy a reassuring look, and got down to business.

"So, that video? It's not *actually* a good thing that so many people saw it. I was with Ruby right before her manager, DeeDee, came to get her. Her dad has her hidden away somewhere." She braced herself for the next part. "The thing is, guys, she's gone, too. She won't be at school for a while, maybe ever."

Both boys were stunned into silence. She took in a deep breath and let it out slowly. Looking down at the treat Carlos had given her, she pushed it away. Putting the rest into words somehow made it more real and Jett didn't want to say it aloud—but they had a right to know.

"Guys, Ruby has something called 'stalkers.' You know, like you see in the movies and on TV crime shows? Some scary people are looking for her and not for good reasons. Because of this video, her dad thinks they could find her and, if not her, then Sam." A single tear fell down her cheek. Her voice wobbled with emotion and she deliberately looked up into their eyes. "What are we going to do?

They're both in trouble now and—and I just don't know what to do."

Carlos squeezed her hand—hard. Andy looked up and closed his eyes, murmuring something under his breath. What *were* they going to do?

Finally, Andy pushed through the heavy silence. "I don't know what we can do," he said, lowering himself into a chair as he regarded his friends. "It sounds like Ruby is safe. She has her family and team looking out for her. But Sam? If we know her and *we* can't find her, do you *really* think someone else can? Why would they even be looking for her instead of Ruby?"

He knocked softly on the table as he thought things through, eyebrows furrowed. "Maybe the best thing we can do for them is also the best thing we can do for ourselves: focus on what we *can* control—and that is schoolwork. Now that Ruby is out, too, I think we need to revisit ideas for the sophomore project."

Carlos exploded. "Andy! Man, you don't care *at all*, do you? Can't you see Jett is on the verge of going silent again and maybe being sent away?" He eyed Andy with deep disgust and what looked to Jett to be disappointment. "Sam and Ruby are already gone, and you're worried about projects?! And here I thought you were Mr. Community!"

But Andy wasn't having it. He lashed back at Carlos with just as much frustration and disgust. "And what are *you* going to do to find them? Score the next winning goal at your stupid game and hope they are at the after-party?"

Carlos sputtered for a moment, but didn't offer ideas.

"That's what I thought," Andy said. "It seems to me that the best thing *we* can do is take care of *our* work so *we* can get them up to speed *if* they come back! Isn't that part of your beloved 'Winning,' Carlos? Taking care of yourself so you perform well for the team?" Andy used fingers to flash air quotes around "winning," almost spitting the word out as he did so.

What was *that* about?

Jett cringed at the hostility rising in front of her. She was used to Ruby and Sam going at it, but she'd never witnessed a fight between Andy and Carlos. Jett wanted to diffuse the tension, get them back to working together, but she didn't know who was right. What was the more important goal, anyway? She couldn't believe their productive problem-solving session had instead turned into a fight!

She buried her face in her hands for a moment as the boys continued to go at it. She wished she had a whistle to blow to interrupt them. Instead, Jett raised her voice above theirs. "Guys! Time out! Go back to your corners and just *listen*!"

Nonplussed at the appearance of a Jett they'd never encountered before, both boys stopped in mid-sentence and stared at her. Jett let out a sign of relief. She had their attention. "First of all, you both did exactly the right things when I was getting overwhelmed, so now I'm still speaking. Let's work with that, shall we?"

The tension of the moment seemed to drain away as they laughed sheepishly at each other.

"We need to stick together to solve the problems we've already got, okay? Then maybe we can work on preventing others later."

Although both boys had returned to their seats, they still weren't saying anything.

"What do you think, guys?" Jett coaxed. "Andy? Carlos? Can we agree to disagree for now and just sort out what needs our immediate attention?"

Carlos relented first. "Okay, 'Manita," he said, dropping his shoulders and shaking his body as if he'd just climbed out of a pool.

Andy looked away, closed his eyes, and muttered, "Yeah. Okay," before turning his gaze back to both of them.

Satisfied that she had kept their undivided attention, Jett filled them in. "Ms. Diaz gave us a few days to come up with a new thesis and I've been thinking a lot about it. None of us needs extra work. And I know you're both worried about Sam and Ruby. I am, too. So I've been thinking maybe we should focus on *safety*."

Andy's eyebrows shot up and Carlos started to say something, but Jett raised her hands for silence.

"I know it may not directly apply to us, but it sure does to people we care about. I'm thinking that will be enough. Plus, we can use what we learn to make sure *nothing* like this *ever* happens again, right? I mean, how many people are truly safe and for how long? Maybe we can fix that." She put her hands down to invite their reactions.

Carlos had been looking down, motionless for once. But at her final words, he had started to nod. Now he met her eyes. "Okay. I can see where this might not add too much extra work, but I think we need to involve Ruby," he said. "I mean, if she's answering texts and all, then it's just that she's not here in person. She should be able to do some of the work!"

Andy, too, had started to nod as Jett finished up and now seemed increasingly eager. "Yes, I think she should. And I like the idea of studying safety. We can use it to help find Sam and to figure out what to do about Ruby's stalkers. But the key thing is that we need to make sure we get all our work done and done well, even if Sam and Ruby can't help much. After all, Sam would be the first one to take care of business, wouldn't she?"

Jett challenged him. "I think it depends on what you mean by taking care of business," she said. "Don't you think Sam would be the first one to go looking for any one of us? Okay, maybe not so much Ruby, but any of us sitting here right now."

That gave her another idea. "How about we compromise?" she asked them. "I promise to keep up with our workload and even help sort out any extra work on our project if you two promise to help me find Sam. Seriously. What if she's hurt? What if she's homeless? What if a stalker gets her instead of Ruby?" A shiver ran through her at that last thought. She swallowed hard as she imagined Sam out there alone, trying to survive, with who knows what in her way. She pinned both boys with a look that silenced them again. "I will coordinate everything with Ms. Diaz, but you two must promise to focus on finding Sam. What if she is seeking safety too, in her own way? She needs us."

Abruptly feeling small and not a little bit frightened, she dropped the fierce look and looked at them pleadingly. "Please?"

Jett hated begging, but she was way beyond so many of her normal boundaries now, and she needed them to agree. Sam was her singular focus. "Just so we're clear here, guys. I'm doing this," she said, gathering her determination around her like a shield. "With or without you, I'm finding Sam."

Carlos gave her an understanding look and pushed the Rice Krispies treat back to her. "Okay. I'm in," he said. "But only if you eat. I don't think you eat enough and I can see I'll need to look after my Manita to ensure she is healthy." He lifted his chin at Andy. "'Migo? You in?

Or will you keep your head stuck in a book?" His glower dared Andy to refuse.

Andy ignored Carlos' challenge and focused on Jett's face. "I'm in and I can help keep us on track," he said firmly. "Jett, you said you'll tell Ms. Diaz about our new focus, but I think we should all go see her right now. This is up to all of us. It's *our* team, our Core5."

Relieved to have them both on board, Jett simply smiled her assent. They *were* still a team—not individuals thrown together on a project to be divided up piecemeal, but a collaborative team working collectively toward their goals, both on the project *and* for their missing friends.

10

THEY HAD DONE it. They had confronted Ms. Diaz with their new focus for the sophomore project and she had reluctantly agreed to their plan. She made it clear that she believed they were in over their heads on this topic, but wasn't that life? To be in over your head and constantly pushing up to the surface to get a breath?

Back in her room, with the door closed and her window open, Jett felt a feather-light breeze teasing her thoughts. She closed her eyes to fully absorb the moment. She loved this twilight time, when day danced into night. Changing colors shifted the tone of everything around her. Jett opened her eyes and studied her boards.

First, she looked at the one about a service dog. She added a sticky note to it that said "anxiety?" and stopped. Was that accurate? Jett reflected on her moment of panic in the cafe, when Carlos held her hand while both he and Andy breathed with her. Could a dog help with that? She wasn't sure how, but maybe that would be something to consider.

Did she even *have* anxiety? Or was depression the bigger problem? She added another sticky note—"depression." Lately, she felt held down by the weight of her life. She felt pinned by pressure and pounded by lack of progress. Jett wondered if her team at the Lodge had mentioned any of this to her parents, which prompted further speculation about what they had put in her file. And just what *exactly* had Daddio shared to convince complete strangers that a service dog could be a good fit for her? She didn't necessarily disagree. It actually sounded too good to be true, because she *was* normal. The team at the Learning Lodge had confirmed that. But maybe they knew something she didn't. Maybe there was something else. Was it terminal? Why wouldn't anyone tell her if she had a specific diagnosis? Why was she left to sort it out on her own?

Next, she looked at the board about Sam. It was empty. She wrote "Ruby" on a sticky note, but immediately crumpled it. She wrote "Grams," but how would she even find her? Jett made a sticky note for Ms. Diaz, even though she had no answers, and on it she wrote "Ms. Diaz?," thought about it a moment longer, and added "Useless." Jett shook her head. She had nothing.

Last, she looked at Ruby's board. Nothing new to add there, either. Did she really have so little to show for all her thinking and plotting? Well, that *was* depressing. No wonder anxiety popped up for her. Jett crossed out the question marks on the sticky notes she had just placed on her dog board.

Grabbing a new board and tacking it to the wall, she wrote SEEKING SAFETY in all caps across the top. She added a sticky note—"Ms. Diaz approved"—and then a second one—"Andy and Carlos on board." Those two were followed quickly by a third: "Ruby remote." The fourth and final one made her sigh heavily as she added it: "Sam still out."

Someone opened the door to her room, stood waiting, and cleared their throat. She jumped at this unexpected noise and immediately felt a flash of anger. A flood of hot irritation coiled in her muscles. How long had the intruder been standing there? What did they see? In the brief moment she had to react, Jett decided it didn't matter who it was. She did not want *anyone* to read *any* part of the internal pain scrawled on her boards. Those were meant for her to examine. Privately.

Jett spun around and charged at the intruder, yelling, "GET! OUT!"

She was glad she had. It was her mom, the last person she wanted seeing her innermost thoughts. Jett got right up into Mother's face and snarled, "Who gave you permission to enter my room? Don't I deserve some privacy? I've earned the right! I get straight A's, I've made friends, and I've been going to therapy with Dr. Williams ever since I left the Lodge! Nothing I do is ever enough for you! When will you let me keep even a *little* piece of my life to myself?"

Caught off guard, her mom took several steps back and threw up her hands defensively. "Whoa, Jett! I thought you'd be happy to know I'm back from the symposium. I thought you'd want to know the minute I returned," she said placatingly—but then she went on the offensive. "I thought you might even miss me, especially knowing I was gone for *10 days* just to learn how I can help you! Not some random client, but my *own daughter*. And *this* is the greeting I get?" She shook her head, looking sad. "Dinner is ready, but first we need a family meeting. There is a *lot* we need to talk about. See you downstairs in the family room. I'll go get your father." Mother walked away, back stiff and head erect, like a queen having dismissed an unruly subject.

Jett was shaking. Whether from rage, fear, adrenaline, or anxiety, she wasn't clear. She walked back to the board on dogs and added a new note—"Strong reaction & emotions"—before reluctantly heading for the stairs. Jett knew she needed help *there*. She wondered what waited for her now.

In the family room, Jett found her parents sitting together on the leather couch, quietly talking. It looked intense. She wondered how much trouble she would get in for eavesdropping and waited by the doorway, finding it ironic that doorways were now an undedicated but decent place for lurking. Was it that way in every household?

Daddio looked up, caught her eye, and beamed. "*There's my girl!*"

Jett smiled back. She was so grateful for him. She knew he was always in her corner. Even if he did or said the wrong things, Daddio obviously intended to be loving, so it made it easier to forgive his fumbling. Unlike her mom. With Mother, Jett felt like she was always trying to earn love, to prove her worthiness for it. That made it a whole lot harder to trust Mother's motives.

"Hey, Daddio," she said. "Hey, Mom," she added, listlessly. If she could only give Mother the benefit of the doubt, maybe then Jett would feel loved and valued. Maybe then she would feel—safe.

"You should know, I'm *very* disappointed. How you treated me when I saw you working in your room is not okay," Mother replied, her pinched lips white. It looked like she had to force her words through her clenched jaw. "I was home by noon because I was so excited to come home to *you*. Also, I *know* it's a minimum day—your early schedule—because I checked three times when you didn't come home any earlier than usual. Where were you? How long have you been abusing our trust by not coming straight home after school?"

Daddio caught himself in a sigh of disgust. "Now wait a minute, Kat," he protested. "Jett is a super-responsible girl. I'm sure she has a good reason—"

"A good reason?" Mother rolled her eyes as if he was the one being dramatic. "A good reason for what, exactly? This is *exactly* what I was talking about. She hasn't even tried to explain what she's hiding, like where she goes when we trust she's home. And *already* you're defending her."

Mother sat on the couch like it was a throne, rather than a place to lounge and connect. Jett noted how her dad sat in a relaxed position, open to discussion. Her mother looked ready to lay down the law. Daddio appeared to melt under Mother's attack.

"Aw, honey. I know you're just worried about our girl, but I'm telling you, she's good! *Great*, actually! Tell her, Jett." He looked to her for help, and Jett opened her mouth to speak.

Mother was faster. "Yes, dear, please fill us in on where you were. Are you planning another one of your escapades, like running off to the beach?" She puffed out her chest in indignation. "Your actions affect *everyone* in this family and I, for one, expect you to make better choices." Imperiously, she stared her daughter down, managing to look both enraged and smug.

Jett found it hard to control her temper, but she struggled to do so anyway. Mother's unjust attack grated on every nerve. "Well, *Mom*, if you must know, I was doing schoolwork," she said. "I take my responsibilities seriously, and since I have another year-long group project, I thought it wise to spend my time working on it with my team." Jett wrapped her arms around herself, trying to contain the tension building in her body as she stared her mother down.

"So you say," Queen Mother sniped back. "Who can I check with? Give me their number." She pulled out her phone and slid a glance at her husband. "Watch and learn. This is a tool I picked up at the conference for professionals who deal with kids like our daughter." She rounded on Jett and tapped her phone, waiting for a number to dial.

Jett's open-mouthed stare failed to penetrate Mother's armor. "Seriously?" Jett implored Daddio with her eyes, begging him to stand up for her, but he didn't utter a sound. She ignored her mother and spoke directly to him. "She can't be serious. Surely she can't expect me to give her the names and numbers of my teammates. It's like she thinks I can't keep track of my own life—like she thinks I'm *lying*!" Jett shook with the realization. How could Mother still not know she had no game face? Disgust—and a growing sense of loathing—made her want to double over with the shock. Mother watched her every movement, her glare of icy disgust pinning Jett in place.

They both looked at Daddio, who threw his hands up in the air and collapsed onto the couch, looking frantically between them, back and forth, back and forth. "Both of you settle down!" he urged. "Remember, we're on the same team here. We all want the same thing."

"But do we, Joe? Are you sure about that?" Mother was still tapping her blank phone screen, looking like a spider with an insect freshly tangled in its web. "Tell me, dear daughter, what *exactly* do you want that shows *me* we're on the same team?"

Jett thought long and hard before answering. Now would be a fantastic time to lie, if only she could do so effectively. After all, she didn't think telling Mother that she wanted to be free of *her* would go over so well.

"Well, *Mom*," she said, her voice dripping with sarcasm and absolutely no affection, "if you were around more, you would know. I want to be a respected and valued member of this team we call 'family.' If you were around more, you would know I work hard to do my part. You would know I'm smart and responsible, like Dad pointed out." She glanced at her dad for a moment. "Thanks for that." Then she turned back to this wicked witch 'Mother.' "You would know there's absolutely no reason for your derision, lack of trust, *or* wariness toward me. What are *you* hiding that has gotten you twisted in such a faulty hypothesis?"

The eyebrows on Mother's face lifted halfway to her hairline in surprise. Maybe Jett's self-defense abilities were better than she thought. The real question, though, was why was she having to defend herself at all? And with Mother, no less! If this was supposed to be a family, weren't they supposed to have each other's back?

Mother recovered from her surprise with a nervous laugh and a wave of her hand. "My, my, little Jett. It looks like teenage angst has taken over my sweet and submissive daughter," she said, suddenly shifting gears. "You know her, right? The one who understands I just spent several days and nights of my life at a conference so I can better prepare her for this world? My daughter has to navigate society with disabling conditions."

"Disabling conditions?!?" Jett's mind felt assaulted by the awful phrase. She examined it from every possible angle. Disabling conditions—Plural? *What* "conditions"? How was she not functioning? How was she disabled or impaired or limited in any way? Mother thought she was *broken* and needed to be *fixed*?

Jett closed her eyes, tucked in her chin, and held up a hand. "Hold up here. You think I'm *disabled*? As in *broken*? As in **im**paired? You. Are. WRONG. Let me get you a dictionary" She felt herself trembling with the incongruity of sinking shock and boiling rage. She turned to Daddio, who looked beaten and sad. "Dad? Daddio? My one and only hope? Tell her! Tell her I am SO *not* broken!"

Daddio twisted his hands helplessly as he looked up into her face. Jett saw tears in his eyes and it felt like she had taken a blow to the back of her knees. Dazed, she realized she could no longer stand and fell into the nearest seat. Is that what they *both* thought? Is that how her dad justified getting her a service dog—because she was *disabled*? Tears started streaming down her face. Jett didn't bother to hide them. She wanted to run, but made herself stay. She had to know.

Daddio got up and moved to sit right next to her. He took her hand. "Bug. Doodlebug, my Lovebug, Bug-a-boo." He tried to get her to look at him, but she just couldn't. "Let's listen to your mom for a bit, okay? Let's hear her out." Finally, he caught her eye and nodded encouragingly. She didn't respond for what felt like an eternity—and then she remembered to breathe. She grabbed the hand holding hers and squeezed it. Locked together, they both turned towards Mother.

Still sitting regally, Mother wore a look of triumph. "Well, it's *about* time! Thank you, God. Do you understand now?" She looked with pity on her daughter. "I don't want to be mean or anything. I'm trying to be sensitive, but we've sheltered you long enough. You want to be a valued and *respected* member of this family? Well then, we need to start off with the truth."

Jett felt as if she'd fallen into a deep, dark well. Mother's face peered down at her from the top of the dank walls. Her smug righteousness pushed Jett deeper.

"That's right. The truth," her mother smirked at her. "Well, here it is. I've spent the last *year*—ever since you came back from that hippy-dippy, over-entitled, labels-aren't-the-person nonsense—trying to educate myself so I can educate *you* and your *Daddio*." Jett didn't have to listen for the eye-roll implicit in her tone; she saw it. "I did all this so I can do my part in this family to make up for what *you* lack, Jett. I take it your father never told you that the team from that place gave you a diagnosis?"

They did? And Daddio knew it? Jett felt a growing sense of betrayal stacked on top of the confusion whirling around her.

Mother seemed almost triumphant as she crowed out the rest of it. "That means if you spend time at the Learning Lodge or any place like it, they gave you a formal medical diagnosis and you, Jett, *are* DISABLED. That's not me making up the rules. That's the truth. Whatever diagnosis they gave you, it means you fit in a category, and not one like freshman or sophomore or valedictorian. Are we clear? Do you understand *that* much?"

Jett just wanted to get this over with, so she nodded mutely. Whatever else Mother said, she now understood that her mother had proof to back up the idea that Jett was broken. She felt her father squeeze her hand gently and peeked over at him. Daddio looked like someone had punched him in the gut. Hard. He must be so ashamed of her. She squeezed back, wanting desperately to apologize to him for being broken.

She felt her body shrinking in on itself. Jett felt the withering, the withdrawal, the abject horror of knowing that everything she thought she knew, from the Lodge and afterward, was a lie. She *wasn't* normal. She would have to reexamine how to exist and fit into this world all over again. How had she been so fooled? Looking up into Mother's face, Jett thought she might have seen a softening there. Maybe her mom knew she was finally getting it.

A text interrupted her spiral. Jett looked down at her phone. It was Andy adding to the team thread.

> Where are you, Jett? See you soon?

She wanted to respond, "not today." She wanted to say, "I can't. I'm broken." But that would not do. They had work to accomplish. If Jett was anything, she was reliably productive. And so she needed to go. Should she ask permission? Maybe that would help Mother accept her as not quite so—impaired.

"Um, Mom? Dad? The guys. My team. We're supposed to meet up now and work on our project," she pleaded. "Can we finish this later, please? I don't want to be one of those people who makes a commitment and then doesn't show up. You taught me better than that."

Her dad was nodding his permission. Her mom was shaking her head with an emphatic "no." Who was she supposed to obey—the one who agreed with her or the one she was afraid to keep disappointing? She stirred uneasily in her chair, waiting.

Mother's eyes shifted warily. "I noticed you said 'the boys.' What happened to the girls? At your age, it's dangerous to be alone with boys, especially a *group* of boys. No. No way. Most girls already know this, but apparently, I need to spell it out for you."

Jett tried hard to not roll her eyes. Really, really hard. She tensed her muscles and tried to hold the emotions in, but they were like a pressure cooker gathering steam and she was certain some would escape—and that it would be messy—if she didn't release the pressure soon. She had to go. Now.

She glanced back at her dad. He had stopped nodding.

"As I was saying," Mother added, leaning in to catch her eye. She made a point of it, which made Jett very uncomfortable. "... It's not a good idea. You'll just have to let them know your parents are home and we need time with you. You don't have to tell them that we have to explain how the world works—boys in particular. Maybe you can just say something like, 'My parents and I have plans. Sorry, I forgot.' That should work."

Wait. What? Jett shook her head, trying to dislodge the nastiness that bloomed from seeds Mother planted. Impossible. She picked up her phone and looked at her messages again. The boys were waiting. They were counting on her. This was her work with her team. It influenced not only her present but also her future. She couldn't let Mother's misbegotten fears override her responsibilities. But she couldn't defy her mom to her face. She would have to wait. Jett sent a text to Carlos and Andy.

> Sorry, guys. I'm not feeling well.
> Actually, I'm feeling horrible. I promise to do my part, but I just can't come tonight.

Her phone lit up with responses. Andy was first.

> Oh, Jett. I'm sorry. I didn't know. Tomorrow after school—can I bring you to my Dadi so she can feed you and make you better?

Carlos was next.

> Nita! Aye! Pobrecita! My Mamá can make you something too. Let me know where to bring it. I will have my cousin drive me over.

Jett couldn't help but smile at their concern even as bile coated the back of her throat. She felt bad on all levels. Now she really couldn't eat. She responded.

> Thanks, guys. I'll be okay. I'll see you tomorrow.

She turned her phone off and waited for more of Mother's "truth" to devastate her.

11

SEVERAL DAYS LATER, during the drive to school, Jett told Daddio what she wanted. "After school today, I want to go to Andy's house." Expecting some resistance, she was encouraged when he simply nodded and kept driving. "His family has invited me. I already know our route. From school, we'll take his usual rideshare to BART, then another to his home. Please? I'll give you the address. After work, can you pick me up from there?"

Slowly, Daddio's entire face lit up. He knew being invited over to a friend's home was a big deal, *especially* for the first time. How could he say no? "Yes! Of course you can go. Don't forget to text me the address and I'll come as soon as my workload allows."

Jett felt relief wash over her and she beamed at him. "Thanks, Daddio! Please don't tell Mom. I want to wait to prove I can be a good guest first."

He nodded. "Okay. That makes sense. No reason to borrow trouble."

Jett couldn't wait for school to end. And she hadn't even arrived yet.

WHEN ANDY AND Jett got out of the rideshare and entered the bustle of Montgomery Street, she felt the assault of the city's chaotic sound. Jett strained to see through the drifts of fog obscuring the people in front of her. Nearby, a blaring horn sounded. Jett jumped and refocused. She followed Andy closely.

Entering the underground BART station, she encountered a new kind of chaos. At first, the frenetic hub of decisive action fascinated her. But unlike on the street above, this space was confined and closed in, as if she were sealed inside a Tupperware container. It felt like worn dreams and soured hope. Jett couldn't wait to get out of there. Andy seemed oblivious and just kept talking. Was he doing this for her benefit so she wouldn't focus on all the grime and filth? The olfactory assault on her nose and the sensation of her soles sticking to the floor as she walked didn't really allow her to ignore it.

"And so my sister went, 'Anand, you must—'" The wail of a nearby saxophone drowned out Andy's voice impression. Jett moved even closer to him. She loved his impressions, especially of his sister, and Jett was looking forward to meeting her.

Although Jett had never been on the Bay Area Rapid Transit system before, Sam had told her about this shadow world. According to Sam, some people actually *lived* down here, and Jett watched as a few emerged from their hiding places to entertain and earn their keep. She had forgotten about these performers. Would they know Sam?

Even after she'd absorbed all the stories from Sam and Andy, this underground world was very foreign. She had treasured the glimpses into another life that their stories had granted her, but hearing about it was a far cry from experiencing it herself. Butter yellow tiles covered the walls and the mixed concrete-and-tile floor was littered with remnants of life. Jett watched people passing through the station without so much as a glance at the world around them. Many were moving so quickly, she couldn't count them all. Could they really just ignore this cacophony of sights and smells and sounds that were quickly overwhelming her senses? She needed air, fresh air. And silence, blessed silence. Oblivious to her growing agitation, Andy kept walking. He led her along, knowing exactly where he was going without giving it a second thought.

Suddenly Jett stopped, captivated by a beautiful, soulful, magical sound. Eyes wide in recognition, she followed the voice. Jett felt the song calling her, caressing her soul, wrapping around her like a cloak. Without thought or direction, she followed its pull on her heart. She had to get to the source of the sound before it ended. What if it was Sam? Jett's surroundings were now once removed from her focus, but she tuned back into it just in time to see Andy realize that she was missing from his side. She saw him start to panic. Should she go to him? She knew she probably should, because that's why she was here—to spend time with Andy. But the purity, the magic, the *emotions* woven into the song's melody pulled her away from him. It was like that first day when she found Presidio Prep's music hall and witnessed Sam singing her soul out of her body. Could this siren's call be Sam? Of course it could! Jett knew it. It *was* Sam. It had to be.

Jett started running toward the sound as she heard Andy bellow like never before. "Jett! Stop! *I'm losing you!* Seriously, just wait! I'm on my way!"

And she did stop, torn in half between Andy, who was looking for her, and Sam, who was not. Toward which friend should she turn? Warring options kept her frozen, rooted to the spot. If Andy caught up to her, could she trust him with Sam's secret? Would Sam ever forgive her? She had been quite clear in her demand for secrecy. She made Jett promise. Besides, Sam's story wasn't Jett's to tell. Besides, what if the singer wasn't Sam? Jett felt compelled to know one way or the other. Maybe she could make it look like she'd found Sam by accident! That's all this was anyway— serendipity, a complete surprise. And if it *was* Sam, maybe they could entice her to come back to their world.

As Andy caught up to her, Jett realized it was time to choose. *Now.* But she was torn between their first actual shot at finding Sam and her promise to keep Sam's secret. She couldn't do both.

"Hey Jett, where are you going?" Andy said, panting with exertion as he reached out to touch her arm. "You said this is your first BART ride, so I thought you would stick by me and we would just go the way I know, but then you took off. What's up with that?" Jett heard frustration and confusion in his voice as he gave her a piercing look like he was trying to figure her out. She better come up with something quick.

"I'm so sorry, Andy. I just—I heard this amazing music and I wanted to see where it came from." She gestured in the direction she had been headed, realizing that the sound had faded away. All right, she though. The decision had been made for her.

Relief and understanding flooded over Andy's face, and he broke out into a beautiful smile. "Music, huh?" He peered down the corridor and nodded. "I totally get that. Sometimes I hear this one lady sing and her voice haunts me. I love it so much. But I can never find her. She stops when I get too close and it's like she's a ghost or a figment of my imagination or something, but I just—I'm drawn to her song. You know?"

Tears filled her eyes as she felt his acceptance. She knew what he was talking about, but crying? She didn't want to. Not here. Not now—but Jett wasn't able to rein the tears in. She saw his smile falter as they ran down her cheeks. He didn't understand just how much she understood what he was talking about. Did Jett know the pull of that song? Why, yes, Andy, she did, and she knew who created it. But from what he had said, she also knew she couldn't tell him. Instead, she cried—at the pain, at the loss, and at her withering hope.

Today would not be the day they found Sam.

Andy tentatively reached out his hand for hers. She readily took it. He grinned again, but this time shyly, still disconcerted by her tears. They turned together and slowly made their way to the train. With her other hand, Jett wiped away the last of her tears. They were back on plan. Jett was going to Andy's home to meet his family. Just Jett—without Carlos, without Ruby, without Sam.

And all the way on the train, Andy held her hand like she was worth holding onto. Jett liked this. Every once in a while, she caught him sneaking glances at their hands meshed together, but neither one let go.

12

JETT HAD HAD the best time. She was aware that this was the first time she had been invited to the home of a friend that she had made herself, not her parents' friends or peers, but her *own* friend. So, today was monumental. If only she could block out the relentless ache to find Sam, today would have been even better than monumental. It felt perfect. Jett knew that when she arrived home, she might be in for the wrath of Mother, but Daddio promised to cover for her. They were planning to come up with a cover story on the drive from the Upper Rockridge Hills of Oakland to their neighborhood in Tiburon on the other side of the Bay. There would be plenty of time during the ride.

She expected Daddio to be early. His strategy to get ahead of the traffic came as no surprise. And although she hated to go, Jett was excited to see him and tell him all about this milestone.

She turned to Andy and his family, all seven of whom

were squeezed together on the top steps to say goodbye. She saw three generations of love and respect gathered into one cohesive whole, laughing and smiling as they jostled for her attention. Each person was unique and vital to their teeming circle. Jett realized with a flash of inspiration that she wanted to be a part of a family like that one day.

"Thank you so much for having me over," she said to Andy's Dadi in the most polite voice she could muster. "This was my first time, but I hope it's not the last. I really, really enjoyed every minute. Dadi, no one can cook like you! Have you thought about opening a restaurant?"

Dadi, her weathered body wrapped in vibrant hues of cornflower blue and amber gold that matched her personality, flashed a beatific smile. Her eyes lit up and she took a step forward. Somehow she tinkled as she moved. Was it the bangles on her wrist or something near her feet? Jett couldn't be sure, but whatever it was, she was entranced. Delight danced into her own movements and she swayed once from side to side to see if she could get Dadi to produce the sound again. Dadi leaned forward and reached out with a hum of approval to hand Jett a going-away basket of handmade treats.

"Thank you, Jett. My restaurant is here and is always open for you," she replied, putting her hands together and bowing her face slightly behind them. She turned to Andy and instructed him sternly to bring Jett home with him again soon. "She needs to eat more and I like having her here," she told him, chortling with pleasure as she surprised Jett with a quick hug.

Andy's face flushed with embarrassment, but he nodded respectfully and promised to bring her again soon. Jett liked the way he listened to his grandparents and made time for his little sister, even with her present. They had colored, played endless games outside, and laughed throughout everything. Oh, how they had laughed! She'd laughed until her sides hurt and tears leaked. They cheered when Anamika made up a dance routine on the spot. Little sister decided all three of them had to perform for the grown-ups. Jett had been awful, stumbling clumsily over her assigned moves but laughing and smiling throughout, which garnered more mirth. And, thankfully, Andy hadn't been shy about joining in and trying to explain to her how to follow the steps. From observing sibling interactions in the movies, Jett had expected some angst, but there was none, at least not today. The moment his little sister had asked him, Andy had jumped right in and followed her lead. This gave Jett permission to do the same. It was a memory she knew she would always cherish.

As Daddio pulled up in front of Andy's home, Jett waved goodbye to the family crowding around her. Practically dancing down the stairs to meet him, she kept her happiness on her face even as she switched her focus to her dad. Jett realized she was looking forward to telling him everything. When had Daddio become more than just a parent? Would Mother ever be a friend like that? Jett flashed briefly on how deliberately Mother tried to share her knowledge and special interests in clothes and "girl" things. But Jett just wasn't interested. Her whirling thoughts returned to Daddio, trying to sort out when he had moved from one role to many. She remembered specifically when he became her attorney, but what about her friend? Her heart was full, just like her belly.

Oh. My. Goodness! She *loved* the savory comforts of khichdi and idli. Andy had said each family made their khichdi, a staple in many homes a little differently, and idli was "just" a rice cake, but he was wrong. It was *wayyy* better. And *soft!* Not at all like the cardboard discs her mom snacked on. Dadi really knew how to cook! Jett wished her grandparents, who seemed to live completely independent lives, were closer and cooked for her, too. But both sets of her grandparents were so removed, she wasn't even sure any of the four *could* cook. She wished they did. Or at the very least, she wished Mother would cook. Weren't moms supposed to cook? That's how it was on the old TV shows her parents loved watching. And if the mom didn't cook, the dad certainly did. But not in her home. Mother was obsessed with the British Baking Show and liked to try baking. She was actually pretty good at it, but everything else came pre-made. Jett was grateful for delicious food no matter how it got to her, of course, but she also wondered what they would do if they didn't have the budget for take-out and dining out, like Sam's family. Did Grams cook? Oh, that's right! Sam's Grams worked in a local diner in Oakland. Jett experienced a thrill of excitement to have remembered that. Maybe, if she could get to the diner, she could find out if Sam had transferred to a school in Oakland. If only Jett knew where she went to school *now*, she could let go of the constant worry surrounding all thoughts of Sam. Surely she hadn't just dropped out of school. She was way too smart for that, and super-smart kids didn't just give up on their education, right? Even uber-famous ones like Ruby didn't drop out! So, surely super-talented, super-smart ones—

"Jett? Earth to my Lovebug!" Daddio's friendly voice reached into her whirling brain. She realized with a start that she'd been completely ignoring him from the moment they'd pulled away from Andy's house. They were already on the freeway! "Wherever you've been, sweetie, it's time to come back now. We have to get our stories straight before we see your mother."

She smiled sheepishly at her dad. "I'm so sorry! You're absolutely right. I was just thinking about this amazing day!" she explained quickly. "So—do you think Mom will buy that I went to your office and hung around while you finished up your case work? It's not *too* out of the ordinary, except I didn't get much done. Was Uncle in today? Do you want me to text him about our plan in case she checks up on me?"

Daddio sneaked a peek at her and gave her a sly grin. "Good thinking, my girl," he said with a hint of admiration. "I should have thought of that! Yes. Please text him from my phone. Tell him you're typing for me, but I said that he's to act as if you came into the office straight after school again and pretty much just stuck to yourself. He's not even sure anyone else knew you were there. That's how well you blend in."

Jett finished typing on her dad's phone and sent it off. "And sent! Should I erase that part of your text conversation once he responds?" Daddio laughed ruefully and cut his eyes at her. "Again, good thinking! Wow! You're going to be a master strategist someday." He was grinning widely.

She felt moved by his vote of confidence. He really was so much more than just a parent to her. She smiled back at him eagerly. "Thanks, Daddio! I wouldn't mind growing up to be like you," she said. "I think that would be cool, helping others by defending them. But what do you do when someone asks you to do something you don't want to or you no longer think is in their best interest? How do you handle that?" Jett was thinking about Sam again. She was *always* thinking about her best friend.

"Whoa, Jett! You did it again!" Daddio let out a low whistle of admiration. "Do you know you just asked a third-year law ethics question? Are you sure you're just 15 years old? Maybe we should skip school and just start prepping you for the bar exam. What do you say? Up for it?"

Jett loved his teasing but waited for the answer to her real question. When he didn't follow through on that, she pushed him a bit. "Um, Dad? Seriously, I want to know. How do you work through what to do when your client makes you promise to do something, but then, as things progress, you have to choose between keeping your promise or looking after their best interest? Is there even a question or do you just keep your original promise?"

He quickly glanced at her and then refocused his eyes on the stop-and-go traffic in front of them. In the Bay Area, you had to keep vigilant while driving. "For real, then? Well, I have to keep my word to my clients. I would explain to them what I wanted to do and why, but ultimately I would have to do what they want. But if they're a friend or family member—even if they'd hate me afterward—I would look after their well-being over my reputation for never breaking promises. To me, the higher promise is loving them and that's what I take on when I care about someone." He silently chewed his lower lip for a moment. "Does that help, Bug?"

Jett pulled on her seatbelt as she thought it through. "Yeah, Dad. It helps. It hurts, but it helps too. Thanks. Can I ask you another question?"

"Sure, kiddo. What?"

"Well, I'm pretty sure from what Mom said the other night that she thinks I'm not normal. She wants me to admit I'm broken or something so she can fix me." The memory of Mother's betrayal still stung deep in her heart. "But I *know* I'm normal. I mean, I know I'm not *her* normal, but that doesn't matter because normal isn't comparative—right? My entire team at the Learning Lodge and Dr. W and I—we can't *all* be wrong on this and Mom right, even if she thinks she has backup."

She shifted in her seat, looking at the side of his face as she got to the key question. "But *is* she actually right? This doesn't seem like one of those things where we can both be right. So, who *is* right?"

She could see that he was taking her words very seriously. After he hadn't said anything for a long time, she took a quick breath, as if she was about to speak again. Daddio held up a finger to let her know he was still thinking. As he continued to cogitate, he shook his head and sighed. Without a word, he took the next exit and pulled into the first drive-through. Still not even looking at her, he ordered two vanilla milkshakes. Jett watched mutely, confident that Daddio had some kind of a plan in mind. Once the order was handed in through his window, he passed the contraband—Mother would have a fit if she knew about this unexpected treat—to Jett and merged back into the tangle of traffic. Joe Harper waited until they were safely merged back onto the highway and doing the commuter crawl before he spoke. He kept his eyes on the road straight ahead as he finally did so.

"Kiddo, I love you. You are the light of my very existence," he began. "You're gonna have to trust me that your mom loves you, too." He held out his hand and Jett passed him his milkshake. "Don't rule her out just yet. She spent almost two weeks at a professional conference hoping to learn more about how to be a better mom to you. I know you can't always see it, but she just wants you to be happy. In her own way, she works really hard toward that. Sometimes she gets caught up in what she knows—in how she sees the path to happiness—and she forgets that there are many paths up the mountain, many ways to reach the same spot."

Jett started to interrupt, but he held up a finger again before taking a long draw on the thick shake. She tried to stay still, but her fingers started dancing as her leg bounced up and down.

"Learning Lodge is a revolutionary prototype of groundbreaking medical treatment for the brain," he continued after he swallowed. "They focus on synthesis, on how the brain works with the rest of your system. I can assure you that they are *not* some hippy-dippy, fly-by-night place of mumbo-jumbo. Remember what they taught you: Normal is subjective and limited to only one experience. It's *typical* that is comparative. Therefore, it's entirely possible to be normal and typical as well as normal and atypical."

He took another long draw on his shake, swished it briefly in his mouth, and swallowed before glancing over at her briefly as traffic came to a standstill. She'd rarely seen him look so serious; it was clear he had more to say.

"None of that means you're broken—because you are anything but that," he said, his voice shaking slightly. "I hate that *anyone* can paint you that way and that you get put in a position of having to accept your brokenness, even when you know you aren't." Even though she could only see one side of his face, she could tell that he was deeply moved. "What I want you to accept is your awesomeness, your uniqueness, and your own path up the mountain."

As she tried to take it all in, her fingers drummed a rhythm on her thigh, as if they were typing everything he said into her very being.

Daddio took a big slurp of his shake, shook it, and frowned.

"Now, here's the hard truth. Your mom may never be close enough to you on this mountain to walk beside you. I don't know that she can change paths any more than you can—or I can, for that matter—but I do know that you can cheer for others who are on different paths, especially when they are going in the same direction as you."

For a few moments, he beat a rhythm with his palms on the steering wheel that matched what she was doing on her leg. When he stopped, he took in a deep breath, held it briefly, then let it out long and low through his nose.

"It's a choice you can make. Some people are so happy with their path that they want everyone they love on the same one. But it doesn't work like that, does it, Boo? That would be typical." A look of profound sadness washed over his face—and then disappeared. "I also know that being atypical entitles you to extra tools so you can get where you want to go, like a service dog, if one will help you. And I think from what I've seen in the past, a dog may just be able to help you."

After being mute for so long, Jett had to clear her throat before she could speak. "Okay. But—" She stopped and coughed again. "If I accept I'm not typical, am I saying I'm disabled? Am I agreeing that I'm impaired? That doesn't feel right."

Daddio ran his fingers through his hair and lowered his voice to a gentle timbre.

"Sweetie, let me pull over. I want to ask you some hard questions and I want you to think, really think, before you answer. Okay? This is just between you and me." He maneuvered the car silently through the congestion, ultimately pulling off at Strawberry Point, where he found a parking space overlooking the Bay.

He turned the engine off and let out the breath he'd been holding for some time.

"Baby, do you ever feel like you're not understanding something everyone else just gets immediately?"

Jett slowly nodded as she whispered, "Yes. A lot."

"Do you ever get so caught up in what you're doing that you just can't be bothered to stop for *any* reason—like to eat or talk or do anything that requires you to pause what you're doing?"

"Um, duh, Dad," she replied, smiling at him. "Of course I know how to concentrate. That's, like, one of my superpowers!"

"Okay, well, do you ever find yourself unable to manage your own body? It just does things and you don't even know it or you get so churned up, you can't stop moving?" He glanced meaningfully at her tapping fingers, which hadn't paused in several minutes.

"You mean like when I pinch my neck, slap my legs, or bounce like Tigger? You nailed it," she said, glancing down at her fingers but not bothering to stop them. "That's exactly how it feels, like I have so much to express, I just can't stop it from coming out. Honestly, most of the time, I don't even know it. It's like I'm letting all the internal stuff leak out. My body just moves without permission."

Daddio carefully placed a hand over her fingers, stilling them. He waited until he had full eye contact before he continued. "Kiddo, I want you to know you're brilliant and different and really awesome as Jett. But you are never gonna be like your friend Ruby or like your mom. Your normal will never be the same as theirs. Because they are normal *and* typical while you are not. And the whole point here is that's okay. Do you know that?"

She kept eye contact as she nodded slowly and seriously at him.

"Okay, kiddo, then here's some more hard truth," he said, gently squeezing her hand. "Normal and *not* typical is not okay to some people. They only know how to understand and tolerate and accept normal *and* typical."

Jett leaned into his shoulder and squeezed his hand back. He reached over with his other hand and caressed the top of her head. "Kiddo, that doesn't make it right, but right or not, it's real. A service dog won't make you typical, either. In fact, having one is like wearing a big sticker saying you're not, but what a dog can do is help you on the journey to the top of *your* mountain. A partner like that could help you get there faster, better, and with more ease. And that, my heart, is why I am so in favor of you having one, because I'm always in favor of you having what you need."

She squeezed his shoulder in an awkward half-hug before she leaned silently back into her seat. As Daddio turned the car back on and finished the drive home, Jett noticed the changes in his body language. He looked more relaxed. She saw it clearly now. He was the best Daddio ever, especially for how he helped her understand things. She was sad that right and real weren't the same. She was sad to know there may be whole segments of the population that would never accept her because she wasn't typical—including her mom. And she was elated to finally recognize that a dog *could* help. How? She still didn't know, but she believed in her dad and she believed in his love for her. Daddio wanted her to have the very best life. If that included a dog, she only had one more question.

"When can we get one, a dog like that?"

He smiled as he punched the button to open the garage door and pulled in to park. "You're on the list and I've been told it can take a few years. But I also believe the right one will be ready for you at exactly the right time. For all we know, they may even be preparing now. Wouldn't that be cool?"

Jett was so excited at the prospect that she felt as if she might wriggle out of her own skin.

"Yes! Thanks! You're the best. Seriously. The best!" She leaned over and kissed his cheek. Never could have predicted how this day would go, but she liked this part of her path up the mountain. She might not be going up the same path as everyone else, but her way was beautiful, and she was grateful.

13

RIDING THE HIGH of a couple of really productive days, Jett was excited. Finally, she could direct her full focus on her *true* mission—to find Sam. In order to reclaim a bit of her integrity and a sense of self-worth, Jett had to do this by herself. She would ask the boys to go with her to the diner where Grams worked, when she sussed out where *that* was, but scoping out the underground BART station where Sam sang *sometimes*? That was up to her and her alone. This did not change the fact that she hated the grime seeping into her life because of her search.

From the street level, Jett carefully descended worn, slick steps into the Montgomery Street station. She felt the air change. Taking in the sour aroma of determination and debris, she tasted songs unsung and manic mutterings. Jett studied the people rushing by. People moving with purpose intrigued her. They moved at a frenetic pace. Should that be her? She had a purpose. She had a plan—sort of. But Jett had no path. Where would she find Sam? She was just guessing. Right now was the same time of day as well as near the same place when she'd last been here and heard Sam's siren call. Would Sam keep to a schedule? Could it really just be a simple matter of listening? Jett let the mayhem of BART's sounds wash over her, drowning out the sights and smell. She heard a saxophone and smiled. She was getting closer.

Passing rancid butter walls, she looked for her friend. She looked everywhere she dared and worked hard not to go into overwhelm. The fingers of Jett's left hand involuntarily started pulling at the skin near the base of her neck, above her clavicle. The sights, the sounds, the soiled smells demanded attention and bile rose in her throat. She fought for focus, since she didn't see or hear Sam yet. Jett started mumbling encouragement to herself. She could do this. She would—for Sam.

"Hey girly, you lost?" rasped a filthy, stringy man of indeterminate age. Jett turned her head. Was he speaking to her? Nearby, a man with wiry whiskers spoke to the source of the voice she had heard. "Aw, Kicks, leave her alone," he told his buddy.

Kicks shifted from foot to foot, wiping a hand under his nose to catch free-flowing snot. "She looks real pretty," he replied, ignoring the advice. "I just want to watch—maybe touch. You want in on this?"

Jett didn't know how to handle this attention. Would it be rude to ignore them? Should she say something? But they were strangers. Was she in danger? Could she be? Out here, in public, with so many other people around? Should she stare them down? Mother insisted that when someone spoke to her, well-mannered people always made eye contact. Jett wondered if this applied to strangers in a smelly, grimy, strange land. She knew it applied to strangers when she was with her parents. Her right hand started tapping a staccato rhythm of frenetic concern on her right thigh as her left hand picked up the pinching pace at her collarbone.

Focus. She needed to focus. Was she in the right place? There were so many options and places to look down here in the underground. Every tunnel and hallway was connected and yet somehow separate. Jett realized other people were watching her, as if she intruded on their living space. She looked around again. Jett saw no trains, no travelers, no musicians, no performers. All she saw was lots and lots of transients. Why were they called transients when they seemed to go nowhere? What had she stumbled into? Jett's brain started spinning faster. Her stomach roiled. She felt sick. This wasn't where Andy had taken her. This wasn't *anywhere* she had been before. How was that possible? She had a sudden urge to run back to some place that she knew.

Meanwhile, Kicks and his comrade were staring at her, slowly sidling closer. They seemed to be silently communicating. Should she scream? Would anyone come if she did? Or maybe she should just move on without talking to them. She had no idea what to do.

With a start, Jett remembered what she had forgotten. *A ticket!* She needed a ticket to ride the train. Turning warily and feeling a growing need to escape the area, she looked for the row of ticket machines. She remembered them lining the walls in the entry area. Jett also kept an eye out for the guard who should be sitting in an opaque office near those machines. She needed a ticket to feed the gateway near the guard and he would help her if she still needed help. It was his job.

The hairs on the back of her neck rose as she turned away from the men and picked up her pace. Immediately, she sensed someone following closely behind her—in her space. Was it only one someone? She smelled wet, rotten breath as the too-close stranger peppered her with words that hit her skin. This wasn't Kicks. He hadn't followed. This was new trouble, more insistent trouble. Panic crawled up her spine.

"Girly, come here. Come with me. Come, rest a bit. I can help you out."

Something grazed the sleeve of her hoodie, and she screamed. The pressure was too much. She threw up her lunch, splattering vomit on the hand reaching out for her. That caught the nasty man off guard. He backed up and his friends laughed. Jett wiped her mouth with the back of her sleeve, turned, and sprinted toward the rumble of trains. She needed a new plan. This one was failing.

No music. No Sam. How long had it been since Jett heard music? Wanting the soulful sound of the sax, she retraced her steps and was relieved to find the ticket machines. Jett fumbled with a bill, before blindly stuffing cash in and snatching out the ticket it offered up. Shaking, she threw herself into the safety of swiftly moving commuters. She knew she looked a bit off. She also knew she smelled like puke and persistence. People looked at her funny. Was she that obviously out of her element? Did she look like a transient, an underground urchin or some kind of street performer? Maybe if she sang, Sam would find her. Jett swiped at her face again with her other sleeve. Could she just open her mouth and sing? Sam would know her voice. She would come.

Jett breathed deep. She gathered her courage, planted her feet, and closed her eyes. She thought about her lessons with Sam. Sam had said singing meant Jett needed to listen inside, feel all of her emotions, and give them voice. Jett felt herself sync to her internal soundtrack. She opened her mouth and the words from *Get Here*, originally performed by Oleta Adams, poured out of her soul.

When she opened her eyes at the song's conclusion, Jett saw commuters, usually rushing to and fro, surrounding her. Some clapped. Some waited for more. "Where do I put your tip?" one man asked. Jett tilted her head and shrugged.

"Look, I've got time for one more," a woman said impatiently. "Are you going to sing another?"

Jett turned toward her and nodded slowly, knowing that's exactly what she needed to do. She could do that.

Sam hadn't come yet, so she needed to sing again. Maybe one more would be enough?

People passed by as she centered back into her body. More stopped, drawn in by the growing crowd. Jett took a deep breath and gagged a bit on the station's stench. She tried again, but her lungs demanded fresh air. No, she needed to attract Sam. This was the only way. Jett closed her eyes again and opened her mouth. *Every Time I Breathe*, originally by Arlissa, poured out.

When she finished the song and opened her eyes, Andy was there. So were his friends. She watched him wave them off. Ashamed by her failure and feeling exposed, Jett ducked her head and blushed. People were leaving. Some thanked her for her music. Wringing her hands and staring at the ground, at the station walls, at the chunks of dirt in a stairwell—anywhere but at Andy—Jett nodded mutely, bereft of words. No Sam. Yes, Andy, but he looked stunned, and she didn't know what to do next. He hadn't been part of her plan. The wrong friend had come. But he *was* one of her people. Would he help her get out of here? And what about Sam?

A tear fell down her cheek. In her smallest voice, so quiet he had to step forward and ask her to repeat it, Jett asked: "She isn't coming, is she?"

"Who?" Andy quietly replied.

A sob escaped, and she started to melt. Andy caught her by both arms, soothing her with a quiet murmur: "Hey, hey. Tell me."

Jett swallowed hard and let out a gasp of frustration. "She's not here. I thought she would be, but she's not. I thought I could find her," she said, her words picking up speed and volume as she went. "I thought, maybe if I sang she would hear me and she would come, but she didn't." Her tears were flowing freely now, her shoulders shaking with deep sobs.

Andy pulled her into him and hugged her tightly. "Awww, Jett," he murmured softly into her ear. "Who? Sam? You thought if you sang, Sam would just—come? Why? Does she know you sing? Has she heard you before?" Andy looked around a moment. "We're going up. Will you come with me?"

He felt her nodding and took her hand as he released the hug. For Jett, holding his hand was the most natural thing in the world. Andy's friends gathered around, putting her in the middle. None of them said a thing. Today there was no laughing. Jett missed that sound, but she thought maybe the absence of it was out of respect for her. Together, they walked up out of the grime and into the urban world above.

A few steps beyond the station, Andy stopped walking and sought her eyes. "Jett, do you want to hang out with us or do you have other plans?"

Her plan had been to find Sam. That's what she wanted to do and if she couldn't do that, she needed to go. Daddio was expecting her. Besides, even though she wasn't shaking anymore from her underground ordeal, she still smelled gross.

Jett broke eye contact with Andy and motioned toward Daddio's office. "I need to go up there. My dad is expecting me." With a deep breath, she gathered herself a bit more. "Thank you for finding me. Can we talk tomorrow?"

"You bet," he said, beginning to smile again. It was a dazzling sight, his beaming joy.

Jett waved, returned the smile, and walked off toward Daddio's office. She hadn't found Sam, but she had inspired Andy's fabulous grin. She liked inspiring those. Was that what it was like to be a good friend? If so, she could do that. Maybe not for Sam or Ruby, but at least sometimes for Carlos and consistently for Andy. She stopped that last thought to modify it—Anand. Jett wanted to get his name right and start calling him that outside of class. He deserves that; she thought. Glancing behind her, Jett saw he was still watching her as she crossed the street. She raised her hand in one last farewell before disappearing from his sight into the office building. Mixed emotions colored her movement, but she was good. She had a plan, and it was time for the next phase.

14

A WEEK LATER, time continued to move like molasses on ice. With Sam gone and now Ruby too, the increased amount of energy it took to stay focused and keep on her mask of "everything is okay" exhausted Jett. Walking up the front porch steps, she breathed a sigh of relief. She was almost home. Thank goodness the house would be empty. She wanted peace, quiet, and maybe a snack. Thinking back on her missing teammates, Jett was determined to stay connected. At the beginning of this school year, she promised Ruby she would text. That was months ago. Would now be a good time or should she wait a little longer? It *was* almost winter break. Jett pulled out her phone to text while unlocking the front door with her bright pink key. As the door swung open, a crowd of unfamiliar faces greeted her. Time stopped entirely. Phone slipping from her hands, Jett wondered if maybe she had somehow walked into the wrong house. She turned around in a full circle, taking in every detail. Yep. This is where she slept each night. What in the world was going on?

Finally, a familiar face came into view. Mother came at her brusquely, all business and no warmth. "Ah, Jett, honey. There you are," she said, reaching for the backpack that Jett still had slung over one shoulder. She used it to leverage Jett deeper into the living room as she spoke. "We've been waiting for you. Can you help us understand a few things?"

Stumbling forward, Jett's confusion began to clear as she noticed that everyone was dressed like Mother when she was in therapist mode. Was this a group of her colleagues? In their *home*? She inspected the crowd a little closer. A few of the roughly 28 faces looked vaguely familiar. Confusion shifted toward impatience, which she struggled to hide. Did Mother expect her to do or say something? She had asked Jett a question, but it was so vague. Help them understand *what*, exactly? Well, she *was* a pretty good sleuth, despite not finding Sam yet. Mutely, she slowly nodded her agreement. She would help if she could. Mother hefted her Spiketus Rex off her shoulder and hung it up in the entryway before ushering her into the sea of new people.

"Hi, Jett," said an unfamiliar man.

This stranger used her name like he knew her. Wasn't that inappropriate? She didn't know *his* name. How was she supposed to respond? Then she spotted an empty chair in the middle of the room where no sensible person would put a living room seat. She looked around warily. Everything else had been moved, too. Most of the guests were standing or already seated in a circle around the empty chair. She looked for somewhere to move the chair that would complete the circle. Who in their right mind would sit in the middle?

Mother spoke like she was soothing a toddler about to throw a tantrum. "Jett, that seat in the middle is for you," she cooed. "That way, everyone can observe your answers, including full body language. After all, *you* are the expert here." Mother's light grip on her arm became a bit firmer as she steered her toward the chair.

Wait—*what*?! How could she be the expert here? Maybe she could pretend she was a guest lecturer at this gathering, an expert in—what, though? "Um, Mom–" Jett really hoped Mother could be a parent right now and not a therapist. "What am I supposed to be the expert in right now, in this group of your peers?"

Mother beamed at her as if she was a small dog that had just done a trick for the first time. "Yes, these are my peers, local professionals, many of whom I met at the annual conference for therapists specializing in children and adolescents," she said, taking Jett by the shoulders and gently pushing her into the chair. "I want you to enlighten us on, you know—" She cast a glance around the room and rearranged her posture. Her tone rang out in professional presentation mode. "On what it is like to be you."

Jett stared at her, speechless. She swiveled her head to take in the circle, where people either were focusing on her like a lab specimen or fidgeting like they were uncomfortable, too. Jett wanted to fidget. She couldn't believe this was happening.

"This will help us heal kids going through the same things," Mother continued, still presenting. "We can help you be normal and have a typical life, and then we can use these same techniques to help others." Although she looked pleased with herself, Jett noticed that she was also trying to hide an undercurrent of apprehension. "Aren't you so excited?"

Jett clasped her hands in her lap and looked down, studying her interlaced fingers. It was all becoming clear now. This was a room full of therapists—probably well-meaning but definitely misinformed on what it was like to be her. All she had to do now was figure out how candidly she could respond. She didn't want them to "heal" her because she was perfectly fine as-is. How could she help them understand she already *was* normal? Jett was uncomfortable being singled out and put on display, but she realized that she needed to do this to help. Mother wanted it. Jett lifted her head up, looked Mother full in the face, and braced herself for the questions to come. This would either go very right or very wrong. Might as well figure out the ground rules from the start.

"So, how—*exactly*—will this work?" she asked crisply. "Do you have a list of standardized questions? Are you allowing me and these observers to ask for clarification as needed? Can I stop at any time? What are you hoping to learn?"

Mother responded by stepping closer to the stranger who had greeted her so inappropriately a few moments ago. "Jett, honey, we are lucky enough to have here with us a world-renowned expert on teenagers like you," she said, gesturing at the man. "He will lead this session. And I'm sure you can ask questions. We really want to understand your point of view." She smiled and glanced at the stranger for confirmation. He dipped his head in acknowledgement.

This skinny stranger and his furtive movements reminded Jett of a cunning fox. Even his voice sounded smarmy. "Yes, Jett, this is all about you," he said, stepping into the center of the circle alongside Jett. "Do you know what applied behavioral analysis therapy is? Your Mother is very interested in enhancing her credentials to include this specialty."

"I know nothing about that type of therapy, but I can do research if that will help you," Jett replied, hoping to sound cooperative.

"No need. I'm really good at it," he said with a dismissive wave of his hand. "My name is Dr. Loras and, as a matter of fact, that is my main treatment modality. Are you ready?" He stopped as if a thought had just occurred to him. "Can we use a lie detector?" he asked Mother. "Would you like to see if she is lying?"

Mother nodded enthusiastically.

Jett wasn't worried. If this would help Mother trust her everyday responses, maybe one day she would learn to accept Jett at face value, too. At this point, she felt ready for anything.

One small woman standing next to a scarecrow of a man, took a step forward. The man clutched a case in front of his body like a shield. After a moment, he placed the case on the floor next to Jett's chair and opened it.

"This may look weird but I promise, it's painless," Scarecrow Man said. "Most people forget they're even wearing it."

Jett doubted he was right.

The man took out some bands, which the woman wrapped around Jett's torso, tightening them in place with Velcro, before affixing a similar band around the biceps of Jett's right arm. It reminded Jett of a blood pressure cuff.

Gently, Scarecrow Man attached electrodes to the index and ring fingers on her right hand and stepped back. "See? Totally painless."

Hmph. Jett smirked inside. Depends on what type of pain, she thought. Physical? No pain. But emotional? She knew that Mother wanted—no, *needed*—to validate Jett's integrity. But here she was trapping and humiliating her own daughter, setting her up for the worst kind of emotional pain. Jett wondered if Mother ever worried about her own integrity.

"Okay, Jett. Now just relax," Mother said.

Jett wanted to laugh. How was she supposed to relax wearing all these wires and surrounded by more than two dozen strangers?

"This entire afternoon is so we can learn how to help you be more like the girl I'm sure you want to be, deep down," Mother continued in what sounded like her professionally soothing voice. "I want to learn how to understand you, so I can help you. I'm so excited about this. I expect loving you will be much easier after hearing your answers today."

As Jett examined Mother's facial expressions, she could clearly identify sincerity. Mother meant it; Jett could see that. All the same, she felt her heart breaking. Daddio was right. He had told her as gently as he could on the day they first discussed service dogs that Mother wouldn't be cheering for her as they each walked their own path. Well, she thought, taking a deep breath to steady herself for what was to come—sometimes the truth hurt. She might as well offer blatantly honest answers to these questions rather than considerate ones. It's not like her mother's expected outcome of loving her more would happen. How was putting Jett on the spot in the most uncomfortable situation she could imagine going to give Mother any insight into who Jett really was?

Jett realized she had closed her eyes after Mother had spoken with her. When she opened them again, Dr. Loras had taken Mother's place in front of her. "Jett, we are all aware of your diagnosis and ready to learn from you. Are you ready to share your thoughts and perspectives?" His unctuous tone made her feel ill. And she wondered: *What* "diagnosis"? What specifically? She remembered Mother being shocked it wasn't PTSD, but why was no one sharing with her what it actually was? Jett was losing her patience.

"Mind telling me what the official diagnosis actually is?"

Dr. Loras raised his eyebrows in surprise and stammered for a moment before looking back at her mother, who said nothing. Jett added her stare to that of Dr. Loras, prompting: "Mother?"

Mother's brows pinched together and while simultaneously folding her arms across her chest, she pursed her lips. After a moment, she firmly shook her head. There would be no details provided today.

But Jett couldn't let this go. How come all these people were privy to her medical information but it was withheld from *her,* the actual patient?

"I thought you just wanted me to tell the truth, not share my perspective. I thought you wanted to collect data," Jett said, feeling a growing sense of agitation. "And how come you all know my private medical information? Did my parents give you that? How old do I need to be to earn a modicum of privacy about who knows what about me?"

The silence in the room squirmed. She hadn't meant to say anything wrong. Those seemed like fair questions. Jett thought hard; she didn't know everything in her own medical files. How come they did and *before* she did? Wouldn't that color whatever results they were going for? Wouldn't that taint the data?

Dr. Loras cleared his throat, breaking the uncomfortable silence. "We had to know your medical information so we can know which questions to ask and if you are even qualified for our help," he said. "I hope you don't mind."

Still trying to be agreeable, Jett felt herself nodding. But she stopped. "Wait a minute. What if I *do* mind you knowing such things about me? Couldn't you knowing taint the data? Wouldn't *that* create bias in your questions? No one has shared this diagnosis with *me*, but now you know things about me even before I do." She blew out a breath and tried to tamp down her rising indignation, but it wasn't easy. "This doesn't seem right or fair. And what do you mean, determining whether *I'm* qualified for *your* help? You told me you wanted *mine*." She rattled the wires protruding from the polygraph to emphasize her point. "What if I *don't* want your help? You said *you* had problems I could help *you* solve. Let's just focus on those right now. You can get personal after I solve your problem. That seems like a really good deal for *you*."

Mother reappeared alongside Dr. Loras, shaking her head as if she had a reason to be disappointed. "Jett, you're doing it again. Could you please, *just once*, stop for a moment and consider that we may know more than you do?"

Jett was breathing loudly in and out through her nose, scowling at Mother. She felt the pulse in her jaw repeatedly jump. The circle of strangers was staring at her like she was a curious exhibit at a science fair. Her knuckles turned white as she steeled her nerves. She would do this and hope, by some unpredictable miracle, that if she solved their problem, her mom would *then* love and value her. It was possible, right?

But the questioning didn't start where she had suggested. Instead, they dove right into Jett's thoughts and feelings rather than giving her a solvable scenario or a puzzle to work out or a math problem. She didn't know what to think, except this was not what she had bargained for.

The relentless interrogation continued until Jett was haggard. Sometimes Dr. Loras turned away from her and briefly toward someone watching a monitor and taking notes. At one point, Jett thought she heard him say "electric shock candidate," but that couldn't be right. She thought that only happened to rats in labs. She knew sometimes dogs were given electric stimuli in training. Surely they didn't do that to humans, and *definitely not* to teenagers or children. Maybe she was too tired to hear correctly. After all, she *had* been out all day, at school and in the public eye, before coming home to this awfulness. Jett just wanted to be alone in her room. She was trying to focus, but just couldn't anymore. After nearly three hours, Daddio walked in unannounced. Apparently, Mother had forgotten to mention today's meeting. He looked enraged. Jett tracked him with her eyes.

Joe walked into his crowded home, took one look at his daughter strapped into a mobile polygraph machine in the middle of the living room, and bellowed. "Kathy! Where are you? What have you *done*?"

Red creeping up his neck, he turned to the mass of people. "Show's over folks. Our daughter is *not* a guinea pig and you will stop this mental dissection immediately," he said, pinning the therapist nearest the polygraph computer with dagger eyes. "Take those monitors off of my daughter—NOW! And do not *think* of leaving before I check that you have no notes or recordings from today's torture session. She's *my* daughter! I want contact details and credentials for every one of you. Anyone leaves before I say they can and I will sue the whole bloody lot of you, as well as your parent organization. This is *not okay*."

Jett closed her eyes at long last, relieved that Daddio was home. She didn't understand why he was this upset—what was that about torture?—but maybe they could have pizza for dinner. That always seemed to make him feel better. She watched Mother as a couple of the other therapists gently removed the polygraph's straps and wires. Mother did not look pleased. Jett had seen the color drain from her skin the moment Daddio got home. Why? She'd have to think about that later. Right now, this moment felt heavy, like it was weighing her down internally, to a whole new degree. No part of her felt fully awake. Jett tried to classify it. This must be what it feels like to be bone-tired.

Jett's eyes tracked people's movement in the room. When her gaze returned to Mother, she blinked rapidly for a moment. No mirage. Mother stood there, arms folded and scowling—a pillar in the whirlwind of activity. Could she make this better? Relieve some of the heaviness? In a very low tone, Jett tried to get her attention. "Mom? I'm tired. I bet you are, too. Let's order from Milano's tonight." She just wanted her parents to feel better and for this ordeal to be over. "I know you usually eat salads, but maybe tonight would be a good time for you to splurge. Do you want to try some pizza or pasta?" Jett could compromise with pasta, as long as Milano's included the pizza bread.

Mother stared at her, her mouth partway open, and then shook her head emphatically "no" and rolled her eyes as she muttered "incredible" under her breath. Then, turning to her husband, her tone turned glacial.

"Joe, I didn't expect you home so soon." Her body language shifted into professional therapist mode as she gestured to the person who had been assaulting Jett with so many intrusive questions. There had been no break, as if speed would increase her accuracy. "This is Dr Loras.

He's here to help us." Kathy gestured around the room. "They're all here to ensure our daughter has the very best treatment. You're behaving like a fool. Don't you realize that I've gone to considerable lengths to ensure we could get expert help? Actually, he's the very best."

Jett saw the muscles in Daddio's face flexing, as he clenched his jaw tight and surveyed the room. "Everyone stay right where you are." He walked briskly to Jett, elbowing a couple of therapists aside to get to her. "Bug, come with me." After gently helping her stand up from the chair, he maneuvered her through the sea of strangers toward the family office, keeping an arm around her the whole way. As they entered the office, he looked back over his shoulder. "Kathy, stay with your friends. I've counted them. If one leaves, I sure hope you know which one, because I will hold *you* responsible." And with that parting shot, he shut the door to the office on the stunned crowd.

Jett wrapped her arms around his middle as he pulled her in close. "Kiddo, I'm so sorry. I had no idea."

"Can we have pizza for dinner? From Milano's? And maybe some ice cream?" Jett asked.

Her ear pressed to his chest, she heard Daddio's breath whoosh out with a laugh. "Yeah, I'd say you've earned it. Want to tell me about it?"

Jett nodded into his chest before pulling away. She didn't want him to worry anymore. "Okay, but I really don't know why you're so upset." She tried to imitate Ruby, rolling her eyes, putting her hands on her hips, and wondering if she could get the tone just right. Might as well practice. "Mom has this new circle of therapist friends and they wanted me to help them solve a puzzle and then explain what it's like to be me," she said in a rush, trying hard to channel Ruby. "Of course, they started backwards with questions about me, so I never *did* solve their puzzle."

Unconsciously, she went from channeling Ruby to trying on a Dr. W move. Clasping her hands behind her back, she started pacing. "To me, it seemed rude to put someone on the spot like that, but what could I do? I didn't like being asked so many personal questions. It seemed like they wanted to dissect my brain or something." She put her hands up in an expression of exasperation that was all her own. "I know that doesn't really make sense because they aren't surgeons or serial killers, but..." She rolled her eyes again and shrugged. "I'm just really, really tired now. It was a long day at school and then all this unexpected 'social' time, too." Jett even put air quotes around the word "social," and congratulated herself when she saw Daddio smile at her. "Can we order now? I'm really hungry. I didn't get a snack or *anything* today."

Joe looked long and hard at his beloved daughter. He just kept staring in the oddest way. Jett didn't know why. Finally, he nodded. "Okay, Boo. I'll order up your favorite, but first I need to get rid of all these strangers. That may take me a bit. Do you want to take a nap first? I'll come get you as soon as the pizza arrives."

That sounded good to her, so they left the office together. Daddio escorted her to the bottom of the stairs so that she could continue up to her room unmolested. Joe turned to the throng below as Jett went up the stairs, listening carefully.

"Okay, folks. I want evidence that you have no recordings of my daughter. That means *anything* related to today's interrogation of this minor child: no sound, no video, no notes, no photos." Jett heard him clear his throat and continue in his most lawyerly tone. "What you saw here was not approved by both guardians and I will take *all* of you to court if *any* of this gets out. Meet me at the front door and, one by one, you can leave as soon as I am satisfied you have no contraband and I have your contact information. Are we clear?"

Good, Jett thought. Her lawyer Daddio was taking this on. He would get his way.

AFTER THE BULK of the people left, Jett was lying on her bed, too wound up to fall asleep. She heard her mother, Daddio, and Dr. Loras near the base of the stairs.

"Joe, I don't know if you realize how much healing we can do for your daughter," Dr. Loras was saying in soothing tones. "We can rewire the brain with new neural pathways and help her achieve typical, more or less. I'm not saying it's 100 percent guaranteed, but she has very good odds of becoming normal."

Jett strained to hear more, but the silence dragged for a few beats before her father responded. "Soooo, are you one of those quacks who doesn't understand that normal and typical are *not* interchangeable? Seriously? That doesn't instill much confidence in your ability to do something so complex as rewire my daughter's brain, knowing you don't even have basic definitions down." Jett could tell he had his arms folded over his chest. That was how he always stood when angry, and he sounded angry.

Dr. Loras was sputtering indignantly. "Quack?! Well, I—"

"Are you not used to being challenged?" Daddio shot back. "You realize you're only an authority in *your* circles. There's a whole big world out there that disagrees with you and everything you stand for. I've been looking into you ever since my wife came home from that conference with her head full of nonsense and spite. Neither my daughter nor I want the snake oil you're peddling."

Jett could hear his feet shuffling on the hardwood floor as he paced. Mother was nearly incoherent as she began to rant at him, but he cut her off. "Kathy, you *knew* how I felt. Is that why you ambushed our daughter and didn't talk to me about it? If that's how you're going to behave, it looks like *we* may have some healing to do, but our daughter most certainly does *not*. No. Just NO! I forbid any more of this nonsense. We both need to agree on that or I will take *you* to court and get your parental rights removed so I have unilateral power to choose care and treatment for her. Start looking for a therapist or a mediator for us, because this is gonna get messy."

That was the moment Jett came back down the stairs. After hours of waiting, she wanted to give her expert opinion on herself. After all, she was the authority on *that*, at least.

"Hi," she said, stopping Mother's spluttering immediately. Jett waved as she interrupted them, meeting Dr. Loras' stare and addressing him directly. "Just so we're clear, you didn't hurt me and I'm not broken. I don't need healing. I need tools. I don't think they're the same thing. And because this is my home, too, I'm telling you: You can leave. Now."

She turned her back on him as he blinked and made little choking noises. He spluttered one last indignant retort. "In all my years, I've never been treated so rudely."

Daddio nodded and grinned at his daughter. "Don't let the door hit you on your way out!"

Dr. Loras marched out the front door. It slammed shut behind him.

Jett took a deep breath before addressing Mother next. "Dad told me about the different paths up the mountain. I understand now. I can't cross to your path any more than you can cross to mine." Jett softened her gaze and tried to sound encouraging. "Dr. W expanded on Dad's 'up the mountain' theory. He said we could probably meet in the middle and forge a new path of our own. But he also told me that *that* would mean working *together*, not forcing our agenda or opinions on each other. I want to try. Do you think you could try, too? Could you give up what you think you know to discover what we could learn together?"

Mother looked back to the empty room that used to hold her colleagues. The fire in her eyes turned glacial. When she heard her mom scoff and saw the sneer forming on her face, Jett felt a lump of unshed tears lodge in her throat.

Mother lashed out at husband and daughter with venom and fury.

"Why should I give up everything I've learned? You can't honestly think we could discover answers *together* and collaborate on our views!" She stared daggers at her only child. "My life worked beautifully until you came along. So out of love, I wanted to fix yours. I wanted so much more for *you*," she said, breathing angrily as she gained steam. "These methods are effective, Jett. You can be *normal!* I wasn't even sure that was possible before I met Dr. Loras."

Tears filled Jett's eyes and she swallowed the sharp and sour bile rising into her throat. It stung. She had offered her mom a choice and Mother had made it.

Jett nodded perfunctorily at her mother. "Looks like we've both made our choices," she said, doing nothing to hide her free-flowing tears. "Mine is out of love, too. But it's also out of self-preservation. I'm sticking to my path and picking up tools I can get from other professionals. Can you just—be my mom? And... and love me?"

She watched Mother turn away, trying to hide her own tears.

The doorbell rang. Dinner was here.

ANOTHER WEEK INTO the school year and still no Sam. Maybe they would learn something new today. When she and the boys arrived at the MacArthur Street BART station in Oakland, Jett was pleasantly surprised. It was more like bright and airy Rockridge than smelly old Montgomery. Scratch that. Maybe halfway in between? MacArthur was her third BART station to memorize and it lay somewhere between Montgomery's cloistering underground and the open skies of the elevated Rockridge station. MacArthur station featured filtered sunlight and almost fresh air. She could do this. Especially with both Carlos and Andy at her side.

"Sis, what're you so happy about?" asked a curious Carlos.

This question brought Jett out of her reverie, the smile sliding off her face.

"No. No, Manita. I like it! I like it so much, but I was just wondering—I want to see more of *this,*" he said, gesturing vaguely toward her face and planting a too-big smile on his own that made her laugh. She covered the new smile with her hands.

Andy watched the interplay with amusement. "Stepped in it, did you, Carlos?" He slapped his buddy warmly on the back as he focused in on Jett. "You know, he's right though. It's good to see you smile."

Jett looked at the loony boys and just shook her head at them. She felt she was always presenting her happy mask. Could they tell the difference when she actually meant it? She decided to tell them part of the reason for her genuine smile today—the part they could influence. After all, they *were* everywhere friends.

"Well, part of my smile is because I'm here with both of you," she said, "and another part of it is that I think today could be the day we make progress on finding Sam."

Carlos and Andy beamed at her as they agreed. Jett felt warm and sparkly inside. They were an unlikely pair of guys, but still, they were both her friends. She reached out and took one hand from each. Jett held on. In unison, both boys looked down at his hand in hers, looked across at her hand in his teammate's, looked up at each other, and shrugged. For Jett, this moment of acceptance set the tone. They were literally all connected. She liked knowing that.

As they began to walk, still hand-in-hand, Jett looked up at Andy. "Can you please explain again how you sorted out where we should go? You said you had it narrowed down to two places: Lake Street Cafe and BeeBee's. I'm not doubting your brilliance. I'm just curious. How did you figure that out?"

Andy squeezed her hand warmly as he gazed down at her. "Well, I remember Sam telling me about going to both. She really liked the pies at one and everything at the other," he said slowly, thinking back on the conversation. "I can't remember which is which, but I know she said one of them felt like home. So, I'm assuming that's the one where we'll find her Grams. Doesn't that make sense? I thought we'd go to BeeBee's on Piedmont Avenue first and then we can walk over to Lake Street if we still need to."

This itinerary thrilled Carlos, who was forever focused on his stomach and what he could put in it. "Do you mean to tell me we get to chow down at *two* places? And one has *pie*? Oh, I am so *ready!*" He quickened his pace, trying to pull his two friends to the first destination. "Lead the way, 'Migo," he urged Andy, then focused on Jett. "You like pie, 'Manita? What kind? I like them all! I can eat, like, a whole pie by myself! I'll prove it. Want to time me?"

Jett just laughed happily at him. Andy looked impressed. "Carlos, man, where do you put it all?"

Still holding hands, they fast-walked into the neighborhood. Happy to be led along, Jett's mind wandered off to think about Sam. How could she just disappear? Be completely gone? Why didn't she *at least* answer her phone? This train of thought was more than distracting. It was distressing. Distressing to the point that she could feel herself losing control of her body. What she saw in front of her faded. She couldn't speak. Jett was tunneling again.

What would she do if she had no way to reach her crew, her Core5? Moving from the premise of Sam's scenario, Jett began speculating about what she would do if the ways she'd always communicated with her friends were no longer an option. Why else would Sam not be communicating? Then her brain shifted again, beating herself up for not knowing Sam's home address and not having a backup way to connect with her in case she suddenly wasn't at school, or online, or answering her phone. She *knew* why she didn't, of course. The thought of being cut off from Sam had been inconceivable. Jett always had a phone, even when she had no contacts other than her parents. She always had the internet, even though she was only now exploring social media for the first time. Jett's mind continued to wander as they barreled along the busy Oakland streets. She wondered if Sam was singing in the subway station; if so, how could she have missed her? Jett thought back to when she had screwed up the courage to sing in the station in her pursuit of Sam. Why hadn't Sam found *her?* Lost in a tidal wave of churning thoughts, Jett felt both boys grip her more firmly. What were they trying to tell her?

Her mind started to scramble up out of its fog slowly. Too slowly. They had stopped walking. The boys were trying to reach her. Where was she? What was she thinking? Apparently, the boys needed her. Why? She knew her face was slack, devoid of expression. How long had she been so lost in her own world? Jett wanted—no, *needed* to respond. Through her physical connection to Carlos and Andy, she felt anxiety seeping in. She felt sweat rise on the palms of their hands, making both her hands clammy as well. Jett started dog paddling through the weights drowning her mind. She pushed. Harder. Faster. She had to get to them before this sea of anxiety drowned them. Almost there.

She heard a man say, "Hello? *Hello?*" Jett felt her muddled mind emerging. Still, it felt like swimming through a swamp of molasses. She squinted hard, trying to focus, trying to get back to a sense of the physical world. Her whole body felt tender, but she knew... she knew *something*. What was it? Jett saw someone unfamiliar crouching in front of her. He wore a uniform and boots. Who usually wore steel-toe boots? Oh! A policeman! What was going on? Why was he here? That didn't—

Unsuccessfully, the police officer tried to make eye contact with her. Crouched down as he was, she knew he was trying to get right in her line of sight. "Hey, I've been talking to you!" Impatience colored his tone. He continued, with menace joining the texture of his words. He didn't bother to look up. "Boys, I suggest you let her go. Now. I'll need to see your IDs." The officer looked from one to the other with a hand outstretched as Andy and Carlos looked across Jett at each other. "Both of you. I said *now*!" The police officer stood up to his full height and rested both hands on his gun belt. He frowned, squinting at the connected trio of teens. His hand moved menacingly toward his billy club. "Something doesn't feel right here, and I mean to fix that."

Neither boy had released Jett's hand. If anything, both of them had moved in a little bit closer, protecting Jett and holding onto her even more tightly.

At this, another police officer stepped forward, swelling his chest importantly as he backed up his partner. "Boys, I *heard* him tell you to *let her go!* Are you stupid or something? Why are you still holding on?" He closed in on their group. Andy and Carlos pulled in defensively, shielding Jett from *both* officers now.

In less time than it took Jett to take a breath, the boys were wrenched out of her grasp. She swayed on her feet as her ears were assaulted by cries of pain. Who was that? Jett blinked rapidly, trying to clarify the inconceivable image before her. Both of her boys were lying on the cracked concrete, their entire bodies pressed into the sidewalk like rugs waiting to be trampled. Something was very, *very* wrong.

Big uniformed men with guns held the gangly teenagers in awkward, painful positions. Jett saw beefy hands on top of their weapons. She read terror on the faces of both Carlos and Andy. Andy's glasses were missing. Where were they? She heard an ugly crunch as a third pair of black military-style boots ground them into the pavement.

"Oops," laughed the new police officer, as he dramatically inspected the sole of his boot.

What the—? Why were they doing this? Still incapable of speaking, Jett could only watch, helpless. She tried to breathe deeply, but her heart beat too rapidly. She tried to make a sound, but nothing escaped.

As one officer wrenched his arms behind his back for further restraint, Carlos cried out. Handcuffs strangled his closed fists.

Jett felt helpless. She didn't understand any of this. She heard Carlos using very formal and polite language, sounding more like Andy than his usual jokester self. "Please officers. Jett is special. She is our friend. She is very important to us. We look after her. I think the situation may have appeared different than how it actually is. If you could only... OW!" He fell silent as Jett heard a heavy thud. Andy remained mute.

Jett came roaring back to life, desperate to do something—anything—for her friends. "WHAT ARE YOU DOING?!" Her volume surprised even her.

Startled, the officers jumped. A crowd had gathered. Someone was filming, yet no one interfered. All the attention swung to the girl yelling at the top of her lungs.

"This is NOT right! How dare you!" Breathing heavily now, Jett's face turned red as she screamed at the officers.

"My father's a lawyer. I'm calling him *right now*. He'll make sure you learn right from wrong. That's his job! And you need to LET MY BOYS GO! NOW!"

Jett whipped out her phone as she took menacing steps toward the policemen restraining her friends. The one holding Andy crouched down to help him sit up. The other two officers stood next to a tanned and toned athletic body sprawled awkwardly on the concrete, hands cuffed behind his back. Carlos wasn't moving.

The police officer who started it all, puffed out his chest, ready to defend his actions. "Young lady, you weren't speaking. You didn't make eye contact," he said sternly. "They were holding both of your hands and it looked like you were being restrained between two young men much stronger than you. I was concerned. I had to…"

"YOU HAD TO WHAT?" demanded Jett. "YOU. HAD. TO. WHAT?" Jett felt her body stretched tight. She felt like a metal spring being pulled out of shape. She wanted to curl back in before she snapped.

The officer stared at her without a word.

Just then, a man pushed to the front of the crowd. "Excuse me, but has anyone checked on the boy still lying on the sidewalk? I'm a doctor."

The crowd made room as a man in scrubs slowly but determinedly moved forward. "I work at the Kaiser just down the road, and if it's okay with you, officers, I'm going to check him out. I think I heard his head hit the pavement."

Jett stepped in front of the mute police officers, who were glancing uneasily amongst themselves. She looked gratefully at the muscly man with close-shaven hair in his mid-thirties who stepped in to check on Carlos. "Please do, doctor. I'm afraid they hurt Carlos. And I know Andy can't see anything without his glasses. Can you check on him after Carlos?" She walked over and squatted in front of Andy, taking his hand in hers.

He didn't resist, but his hand stayed limp. Head down, eyes scrunched shut, Andy's shoulders hunched as if he was waiting for a blow.

Jett glared at the third officer, who had destroyed Andy's glasses. "Who taught you manners?" she scolded. "Didn't you have a family to shape your values? When did you become a bully? Or have you always been this way?"

She focused on the onlookers next. She was done yelling at anyone, but she wanted them to think about what they had seen. "I know the police are supposed to help us, but when they don't and instead do the opposite or make poor judgment calls, who holds them accountable?" She waved the hand holding her phone at them, using it to point at the people who had been taking video of the incident instead of helping. "Why are you all just staring at us? What is wrong with *you*?" She tried to stay calm, but she wanted to scream again.

Turning her back on the crowd in disgust, Jett murmured softly to Andy. "Hey, Andy. I'm sorry. I didn't know this would happen. Will you please keep holding my hand? It grounds me, and I need to call my dad." Making the call, she spoke quickly into the phone. She knew he was in an off-site meeting with a client just a few blocks away. Daddio picked up on the first ring. Jett got straight to the point. She was relieved to hear his voice switch immediately into lawyerly command mode.

"Bug, put me on speaker. Am I on speaker?"

"Yeah."

"Good. Listen up. I'll be there in a few moments. I'm getting in my car now. I want the officers, the doctor, and the one filming—someone *was* filming, right? Well, anyone who was filming, I want them all to wait for me." Jett aimed the phone at each subject as he spoke. "Cameraman and doctor? Can you hear me? Please, please stay so I can connect with you. OK. I'm here."

Jett felt a wave of relief wash over her as his car pulled up. Weak-kneed, she sat down next to Andy as her high-powered lawyer Daddio took over. He pulled a notebook from his pocket and started taking down names and badge numbers, asking how long people had been there, whether they had any images to share, and beseeching them to tell their stories in more detail when he followed up with them in the next few days. Jett felt tears of relief flood her eyes when she saw that Carlos was coming to and under excellent care.

As Joe interviewed the officers, Jett overheard the one who smashed Andy's glasses trying to justify his actions. "Mr. Harper, I assure you we are on your side.

We were just looking out for your daughter's safety," he said, waving a hand at Jett. "What would *you* think if you saw a beautiful young girl being held between two—" He hesitated and gestured at Andy and Carlos with his chin. "Two *guys*," he drew out the word accusingly, "holding her tightly, and she didn't answer your questions. How would you handle that? If the roles were reversed and you found my daughter in this situation, I would hope you would do what I did—look out for her and ensure her safety." He put his fists on his hips and lifted his chin defiantly.

It looked to Jett like he was imitating Superman from the comic books.

Bile rose in her throat. This was all her fault.

But Daddio wasn't having it. "Well, for one thing, I would have gathered more information before I did anything else," he said, staring down the police officer. "If the girl wasn't responding, I would ask the boys why and see if their stories matched what I saw. I would *not* jump to the conclusion I needed to rescue her simply because she didn't speak to a complete stranger." He was building up his case now and pointed at the trickle of blood spilling down Carlos' cheek. "I would *not* employ brute force, rip her two friends from her, and hold them on the ground like you did. And I sure as hell wouldn't destroy anyone's glasses and deprive him of his ability to see!"

He made a deep-throated sound of disgust and turned on the other two officers. "What kind of man expects a young girl to answer to someone she's never seen before, especially if she witnesses her friends being brutalized?" All three officers were shifting uncomfortably from side to side as Joe's volume rose. "Only a man high on his own power trip or a bona fide creeper would do such a thing. Which one are *you*? Keenly interested in young girls or high on your own authority?"

None of the trio made a sound. Waving dismissively at them, Joe Harper waited in the heavy silence. Highly skilled lawyer that he was, he didn't need more words to insist the police stand by. Daddio verified preliminaries with dispatch and clarified for anyone watching that he would gladly hunt the offending officers down if need be. He made sure they knew this was not over, but they should leave. Now. And everyone but the doctor followed his instructions. They left just as an ambulance arrived. Jett watched as paramedics joined the doctor to tend to Carlos. After a few minutes and a quick once-over for Andy, they cleared both of her boys to go as long as they were under adult supervision. Gratefully, Daddio took on that responsibility.

Now that the scariest moment of Jett's life had passed, she realized she was famished. As Joe joined them on the curb, she reached her free arm around his waist and rested her head on his shoulder. "Daddio? Thank you. I knew you would fix this. Now I'm hungry. Before all this happened, we were going to go to two cafes. Andy says one has pie and one has everything good. Can you please make that happen for us? That would make me feel even better."

At the mention of food, Carlos' somewhat drawn face brightened immensely, and he readily agreed. Andy, amused at how quickly Carlos had become enthusiastic again, smiled wanly and squeezed Jett's hand in agreement.

"Okay, Bug, but give them a moment," Daddio replied.

She tried to ignore her tummy's rumbling mutiny and, abruptly, she realized that introductions were in order.

"Carlos, this is my Daddio. Andy, you already met him," she said. "Is it okay if he tags along? I really want him to and the paramedics *did* say you need watching. They probably would have *suggested* we get something to eat *if* they had thought of it."

Joe smiled at her and turned back to the boys. "I would love to hang out with you if you'll have me," he told them. "I've got some questions, too, if you don't mind, and I want to let your parents know about today. Will you give me their numbers?"

As he wrote down their contact information, he assessed the trio of students thoroughly. "I'm not finished yet with what just happened," he reminded them. "I am not okay with it, but for now, I think Jett's right. We should all get some food and maybe take a moment to breathe. Just know that I'm happy to defend you. It is my honor and my privilege. Here's my number. Call when you're ready to talk more." With that, he stood up and brushed off the back of his pants. "What do you say? Can we go eat now?" he added, reaching a hand out to help each of the boys up and then wrapping his arms around Jett, pulling her into a brief hug as he helped her stand.

"Sure, Mr. Harper," Andy said, allowing a smile to escape. Carlos chimed in. "Yes, please. I want to know the father of my Manita."

So the four took off in Joe's sedan, trying to small talk, but falling flat. No one took the front seat. The trio stayed hip-to-hip, crammed together in the back seat. No one seemed to mind. Jett thought that, on some level, they were holding each other up. Her body was tense, still ready to flee. Having the boys on either side of her grounded her. Jett conceded that having all of them together, relatively unharmed, might even have been a miracle. She knew when she got home she would need a new board to wrestle with this afternoon's events. Who knew what Beebee's would have for them?

16

JETT KNEW THE moment they walked in. This could be *it*. Beebee's buzzed with all the tinkle and charm of yesteryear. From the curtains to the crew, every detail paid homage to a simpler time. She looked at the clock on the wall. It was late on a Friday afternoon and she could feel momentum building, the electric hum of anticipation. Jett rocked on the balls of her feet. She felt it in her bones. Was this the place she learned how to find Sam? It had to be. For her, the entire world seemed crazy, dangerous, and out of kilter. She needed it to be right. And through it all, Jett never once considered dropping Andy's hand. It was enough that he was holding onto her as well. She squeezed his hand tenderly. They were both shaking.

"Jett, are *you* okay?" Andy asked.

She nodded, immediately turning the question back on him. "I'm sorry about your glasses," she said. "Have you been here before? Do you know what sort of thing you'd like to eat? If not, I could read the menu to you."

He smiled at her anxious tone of concern. "Yes, please." Andy gently returned her hand squeeze. "I've never been here before, so if you could give me some ideas about what they have to eat, I'd be grateful."

"What about your glasses, though?"

"I have an ugly backup pair at home. I'll wear those until I get new ones."

Carlos, who had been studying the menu earnestly as they waited for their table, jumped in. "'Migo! I'm not really so hungry anymore, but I'm still gonna get everything. You want to just share? It's too bad we had to deal with those *cabrónes*! I still can't believe it." Unconsciously, he rubbed the back of his head and rolled his shoulders as if he were trying to shake off even the memory of what had happened.

Joe Harper remained quietly observant as the four were led to their table. Jett was grateful for the plush U-shaped booths. She liked how it felt to have the seat wrap around them, as if they were all one person seated in a big, comfy chair. With so many options on the menu, she hardly knew what to choose. She and Andy dove into a quiet conversation about what to order.

When Carlos laughed, Jett looked at her father. He must have said *something* to make Carlos laugh. She wondered what. "What did we miss?"

"Nothing much, Doodlebug," he said, still chuckling under his breath. "I was just telling Carlos here about that time you insisted we skip eating dessert because your mother ordered a piece of mud pie for you and you thought it was actually a pie made of mud." He and Carlos began laughing anew, but this time, Andy joined in.

Jett shrugged off the laughter easily. She could tell that it wasn't intended to be mean. "Well, how was I supposed to know? You guys like to eat at some pretty weird places," she said, looking at Andy. "I mean, who actually pays to eat from kitchens that cook snails and frogs?"

Daddio shook his head, still grinning. "There's nothing like *that* listed here though, so…" He looked up from his menu. "Did you guys decide on what to get? I'm looking at a burger and fries. Maybe some fried cheese and a milkshake as well." He looked sheepishly at Jett. "Don't tell your mother." Then back to Carlos and Andy. "What do you say?"

"*Que bueno*, Mr. H!" Carlos piped up. "That sounds great! I'm gonna get me the same as you! Tell me more about 'Manita when she was *pequeña*! I mean—small? I'm sorry I missed that. I bet she was *so* funny!"

"Sure, but first explain this nickname to me—Manita," Daddio replied. "What's the story behind that?"

Jett was glad he had asked. She wanted to know too, once and for all.

Carlos looked surprised. "Oh! No story, really. Just, you know, 'Manita, like *hermanita*, like *hermana*, as in my little sister, because you know…" Carlos shrugged. He blushed. Looking Joe Harper in the eye, he nervously chuckled. "Jett's like my little sister, and I love her. I want to protect her and ensure everyone at school knows they would have to come through me to get to her," Carlos announced, pointing at his puffed-out chest. "'Manita just sort of…" He shrugged and flipped both palms up. "It just sort of slipped out and stuck."

As he slowly nodded, Andy was squinting at Carlos, and her dad wore the biggest, beaming grin. Although Jett thought Carlos wasn't making much sense, Daddio seemed delighted, and Andy agreed. Boys were illogical and weird.

"Well then, Carlos, that makes you my son and I want *both* of you boys to know I am proud of you," Daddio said, reaching out and lightly patting them both on a shoulder. "Very proud indeed. Thank you for protecting Jett even when it got you into trouble. Sometimes people, even police, jump to the wrong conclusion, *especially* if they don't take time to gather all the facts." His eyes looked misty and he quickly swiped his thumb under both of them. "I could not ask for Jett to have better friends."

Still mulling over Carlos' revelation about his nickname for her, Jett leaned in toward Carlos. "Okay, but I have a question," she said with a furrowed brow. "Carlos, people don't really have to go *through* you to get to *me*, right? That might hurt and then you couldn't play soccer!"

Carlos, Daddio, and even Andy laughed, and the earlier tension filled with weighty emotions dissipated on the sound. After a few moments, Daddio cleared his throat. "Enough of that. Please tell me about today. Why are we here, and why did Jett say we need to eat at *two* places?"

Jett, Carlos, and Andy turned mutely to each other. Locked gazes and lips pressed together said everything. They definitely had a reason to be here. Who should tell Daddio their plan to find a clue to Sam?

"Come on, guys. Don't leave me in suspense," he said impatiently. "It looks like you really *do* have an ulterior motive. What's going on?"

Daddio was the most trustworthy grown-up Jett knew. After all, he wasn't only her dad and mentor, but her lawyer, too. Glancing at Carlos and Andy, it hit her how horrible it would be if they also went missing. In that moment, she made a decision.

"Daddio, remember how we can't find Sam? Well, we learned her Grams works at one of two places. This is one. And we're here to find her."

"And eat," Carlos reminded them. "I want to meet Grams, find clues to Sam—and *eat*."

Daddio smiled at all three of them. "Okay, then. So we're here to find the illustrious Grams." Sitting up straight, he peered around the diner. "What does she look like? Anyone know her name? Or is this a mystery to solve before we conquer the real mystery?" He looked eager and curious, rubbing his hands together as he considered the possibilities.

While she was pleased that Daddio was on board, Jett sighed with frustration that she hadn't thought of such questions herself. She had just assumed Grams would look like Sam, but older. After all, her sister, Miya, looked just like Sam, but maybe a little older. Sam and Miya could almost be mistaken as twins. Wouldn't Grams look like them? She took a deep breath and puffed it out slowly through her lips, her shoulders slumping forward in defeat. Out of the corner of her eye, she saw Carlos put on his thinking face. He was stroking his hairless chin like an evil genius. Jett smiled weakly. Oh, Carlos! Didn't he know this was serious? Wait. *Was* this serious for him?

"That's an excellent question, Mr. Harper," Andy acknowledged. "I hadn't thought of that. I guess I just kind of thought we would know her when we see her. But how?"

"Know *who* when you see her?" asked their server. Tall and lanky, he appeared to be not much older than the kids sitting at the table. Brilliant brown eyes stared into them. "Hey! Aren't you the ones who were just on the ground outside being harassed by Oakland's finest?" He shook his head in sympathy. "You would think in *our* city—one which is 70% *not* white—that this stuff wouldn't happen to us!" Gaze lowering, his head hung down, he shook it from side to side. Max, the server, took a deep breath before continuing. "I'm sorry that happened and I feel you.

Right here." He thumped his chest and nodded once. "Let me take your order and then come speak with you. Real talk. I gotta know who you're looking for, see if I can help."

Jett felt confused as she considered his interpretation of their afternoon. What was this about Oakland and not being white? How did that come into play? *Did* that come into—

"Hey, kiddo, the boys and I already ordered. Do you want me to pick for you or are you gonna choose?"

The server and everyone at her table were looking at her. Jett ducked her head, set aside her confusion, and decided to reexamine it all, later. "I'll have what Andy's having," she said, nodding in his direction so the server would know which boy she meant.

After a quick scribble on his pad, the server gathered up their menus. "I'll get right on that and I'm gonna look for Lena, too." He walked away briskly.

Jett watched him go in renewed confusion. Lena? Who was Lena?

When the young man returned, he was not alone. "This is Lena," he told them. "She knows everyone. Seriously. *Everyone* over here. If someone is a local, she'll know them."

Looking up into the wrinkled mirror of Sam's face, Jett's eyes welled with tears. Her free hand moved to her throat. She didn't know what to say. She saw Sam—smaller, older, softer, and smiling. Jett would know that smile anywhere. One tear broke free, and she tried to hide her face in Andy's shoulder. She missed Sam so much.

Andy squeezed Jett's hand and spoke softly to Lena. "Are you Sam's Grams?"

The little woman took a step back. She looked at each eager person waiting for her answer with hope written all over their faces and squinted her eyes. "I think I know some of you," she said slowly, before giving Joe Harper a puzzled stare. "But you? You aren't Ruby. So…" She tapped her chin with one finger and tilted her head. "Are the rest of you something called the Core5? Well, at least part of it? I believe I'm looking at Carlos and Andy and Jett!"

Jett wiped the tears in her eyes with the back of her hand.

"Oh, yes. Yes, indeed, Jett! You *are*, aren't you? Here—scoot over." Grams took off her apron and neatly folded it before squeezing into the booth alongside Carlos. "Max!" she called out to their server. "Take my tables. I'm on my lunch break."

Grams reached across the table and touched Jett's hand, which was still holding her throat. "Honey, I'm gonna need you to talk to me now," she said gently. "Sam says you're a fine girl. So just talk to me, okay?"

Jett took a quick breath through her nose and cleared her throat. Her mind was spinning with what Grams' presence could possibly mean. She wasn't at all sure she would be able to speak. Jett closed her eyes and took in another deep breath before mustering the ability from the depths of her soul.

"Okay," she said in a small voice. She knew she had just

agreed to talk, but what she wanted to do was interrogate. She wanted—no, she *needed*—answers. Where. Was. Sam?

Grams folded her hands in front of her. "Well, well. Sam said you all were different. She couldn't explain it, but she said you all are—*different*. I'd say 'determined.' Yeah? Why isn't Sam with you?"

Carlos reared back like Grams had punched him. Andy's brows hit his hairline. Jett couldn't breathe. She thought she was going to choke on the shock. "Wait," Carlos managed. "What?"

Jett's head swam as ringing started up in her ears. Why would Grams think that Sam would be with them? How much could or should they say to her now? She looked at Daddio, eyes pleading.

He swallowed and tried to come to the rescue. "Ms… Grams? Ms. Lena? First of all, I'm Jett's Daddio, Joe Harper. You can call me Joe," he offered her his hand. "How would you like to be addressed?"

Grams grinned as she shook the proffered hand. "You *are* a charmer, Joe Harper. Call me Lena."

"Thank you, Lena. I'm sorry if the kids went silent. I think they're just surprised by your last question," he said apologetically. "They thought Sam might be with you, or that you would at least know her new phone number."

Lena's smile faded into a look of puzzlement as she surveyed the group. Turning back to Joe, she answered cautiously. "Well, sir, I know nothing about Sam having a new number. I don't even use her old one. Isn't that working? She always has it with her," she said, drumming the pads of her fingers on the tabletop. "As for us, my sweet Sam and I talk when we see each other each day or leave notes stuck to the refrigerator. She's been really busy with that current project for school, you know. She said she didn't have much time to keep me company right now because she needs to keep up with these two 'brainiacs.'" Lena gestured at Jett and Andy, but her hand dropped when she got to Carlos. "You," she said, turning her attention to Carlos. "You she calls the player. Are you a player, son? Or should she be calling you a brainiac, too?"

Carlos looked down and shrugged. Jett could tell he felt bad. She jumped in to defend her first-ever friend. "Carlos is a *sports* player," she explained. "He's kind and funny and was my first everywhere friend. He's not a player like one of those break-girls-hearts-on-purpose guys. I did research on that and he just doesn't fit the profile."

Grams smiled warmly at Jett. "Ah, so you *do* speak. Sorry if I got that wrong."

A worried look took over her face as she shifted her focus onto the whole group. "Can you tell me *now* where my Samantha is and why you all thought she might be here instead of working on the project? It's about individual impact, right? She's been working so hard to prove herself."

Jett's mind continued to whirl, sifting through each piece of data coming at her and narrowing down possibilities.

Some were just not realistic, but others were too terrifying to consider. She had to find Sam. She *had* to. Should she further betray Sam's secrets—and to her grandmother, no less? What if she did and they *still* couldn't find her?

Andy stepped in before she could decide what to do. "Actually, we've changed it. We're working on safety now. And—" He swallowed and blinked rapidly. Was he trying to focus or doubting what to say next? "I don't want to get Sam into trouble, but we haven't seen her in months. We've been looking, but without a working phone number, social media usernames or a home address? We don't have any way to contact her unless she just shows up." He cleared his throat and looked down into his lap, embarrassed.

Even when it was hard to concentrate, Jett believed she was getting good at reading body cues from the boys. She squeezed his hand and reassured herself. Sam was not a liar. *She. Was. Not!* She would come back. A break was not the same thing as an end.

Carlos stepped in and looked at Grams apologetically. "This is the first clue we've had that even led anywhere," he explained. "My 'Manita? She's so worried. She's been going *un poco loco*! Can you tell us where Sam might be?"

Grams now wore an expression of deep sadness as she carefully surveyed each of their faces, ending with Carlos. "I'm sorry to say, Carlos, I really don't know. Sam packed a bag just this morning and said she was going to Jett's straight from school for the weekend," she said, turning to Jett, who squirmed under the scrutiny. "She said you two need to work on the presentation."

Grams looked like she might cry. "Was that all lies? She's never given me reason to doubt her before. And I picked up extra shifts, thinking what she said was true. I should call Miya." Worry wrinkled Grams' expression.

No. No. No! Jett heard a roaring ocean of angst and anxiety inside her brain. She felt their rushing waves taking her out and squeezed Andy's hand tightly, trying to hold on before going under. The tunnel of unknown evidence pulled her through. Again. And she was out.

17

JETT WOKE UP safely tucked into the leather seat of her Daddio's car. She turned her head to the left and looked at him. Joe's brow furrowed in concentration. It looked to her like he was fighting more than the evening commuter traffic. She looked out the window at the night sky. Her smile was small and sad. She'd missed another major moment. Hopefully, he'd fill her in. She hated when her body shut down like that. "Hey, Daddio."

"Hey," replied a distracted Joe. Then the shock registered in his voice. He sat up straighter and stole a glance at his daughter. "Hey, Jett! Hey! You're awake! I was worried *sick*. I wasn't quite sure what to do, whether I should take you to the hospital, or what! But you're awake now. Phew!" He kept driving, color returning to the white-knuckled fingers wrapped around the steering wheel. "Can you tell me what just happened? What do you need? How do you feel? Oh, and text Carlos and Andy! Everyone is so concerned, including Grams. I have her home number now, so maybe we can call her later and let her know you're okay. You *are* okay now, right?"

Jett chuckled weakly. "Um, you know you're rambling, right? Is this a thing you do when you're unfiltered? Better not let it happen with clients or in court," she teased.

Her dad let out a breath that sounded like he was just coming up from underwater. "Kiddo—honesty here—what just happened terrified me. I haven't seen you go out like that in a very long time. I'm thinking we should go to the hospital and get a blood panel run to make sure you're okay. Maybe even a full physical."

Oh no. No, no, no! She had so much work to do. They were so close. She needed to know what they found out. "I'm fine! Really! I just want to go home."

Daddio huffed. Jett studied his profile. He looked conflicted. Even without words, he was speaking loudly.

Jett wondered how she could convince him that she was okay. "I want to be home in case Sam shows up, remember? Grams said Sam is coming for a sleepover to work on the project with me. But I went from school to Oakland and with everything that happened this afternoon, I may have already missed her or she could still be waiting!"

Even as her heart fluttered with excitement, the gears kept turning in Jett's brain. "Wait. No. That can't be right. Sam can't come over. She doesn't have our home address."

The fluttering excitement slowed to a languid beat. Jett fell silent as she thought about that.

"Oh no." She started shaking her head in an effort to dispel the truth. "No, no, no." She kept a watch on her dad's reaction, though, trying to gauge what he may want to do. He looked so sad now, too. "Dad? She's in trouble, isn't she? She's *lying. We **have** to find her!*"

Daddio nodded solemnly, his eyes glued to the traffic in front of him. "Yeah, I agree. But how? Where do we even look? She has an entire day's lead on us and it's too early for Grams to report her missing until Sam's a ghost for 24 hours."

A... a *ghost*? Was Sam *dead*?

Jett started crying. "Sam," she moaned.

This was beyond her comprehension. She wanted to be a miracle worker or a super sleuth, like those detectives she saw on TV crime shows. She wanted it all resolved in an hour or two because that's how they did it in Hollywood. But she knew that dream was pointless. She'd lost Sam for real. Caught in the spiral of this tangent, Jett remained silent. Tears fell from her eyes, leaking pain and helplessness.

"Kiddo," her dad began tentatively. "Now, Kiddo, stay with me, here. You said you wanted to go home, but maybe we should go to the hospital. Or better yet, the Learning Lodge. Yeah, that's it. Let's go straight to the Lodge." He stole a glimpse at Jett. "Want to see Gus?" Daddio put on a turn signal to change lanes, rerouting so they could head to the coast.

The unexpected change pulled her out of her spiral. "Daddio, no! I'm *fine*! Seriously. We just need to get home." She tried to think of a convincing argument.

She *did* want to see Gus, though. Why did her dad have to bring him up? Of course she wanted Gus-the-wonder-dog by her side. She wanted him to soothe her, to allow her to run her fingers through his fur, to be a physical anchor as she processed all of this information. Would he have stopped her from blanking out earlier? She doubted she could work on the mystery of her missing friend at the Lodge, though. The staff there didn't allow outside communication for their guests. No cell phones. Her access to the internet would be limited, so—no. She needed to get home. And she needed to persuade Daddio to take her there.

"Seriously, Dad. I'm okay," she continued, letting out a long, slow breath. "I'm sad, really sad. And worried. It's a lot to process, but I don't think taking a break at the Lodge right now is the best way for me to work through this." She saw that her father's face held a pain that mirrored her own.

"Lovebug, I honestly don't know what to do in this situation," he said slowly. "Before becoming a parent, I assumed I would always just somehow 'know' what to do. I mean, I have your Mother and, for the most part, we make these kinds of decisions together. I've always heavily relied on her to help me be a good Daddio, to teach me how to take care of the most important person in my world. That's what parenting is about to me, working together."

He sighed deeply, pulling himself together as he struggled to figure things out. "But now we're not seeing eye to eye and here I am—with my daughter hurting so much her body short circuits—and I can't solve it. I think you should go to the Lodge. But if you won't go there, and you probably *are* physically fine, should I really just take you home? That seems irresponsible."

He let out a long breath as he maneuvered the car into a turnout and shut off the engine. He turned and looked fully at her, agonized. "Where's the manual for this? Someone read me the chapter on how to make it better when your child is hurting and all the kisses in the world, a Band-aid, even a hospital, won't help. Seriously. How am I supposed to know what to do?"

Jett reached across the console and placed her hand over his. "Dad! I want you to know you're doing fine. You've got this. *We've* got this. I know I'm only 15, but we can sort through this together." She thought for a moment. "Let's brainstorm, okay?"

He studied her doubtfully. "First, let's get you in shape to deal with your mysteries. You need to be well, both physically and emotionally, for that sharp brain of yours to stay on point. Right? One step at a time. Your health and safety first."

Jett leaned back in her seat, nodding in acceptance. A long, low hum rumbled from the back of Jett's throat as she dug into her thoughts. "Okay. Here's what I'm thinking. First things first and that's physical safety. What if I promise not to go anywhere without someone who knows how to reach you immediately? That way, you won't have to worry when we're apart. Also, what if I promise to check in with you before going on after-school adventures like today? Does that cover it?" She waited anxiously for his response.

Daddio ran a hand through his hair as he considered her proposal. "That sounds like it would work. It would help me keep you physically safe." He locked eyes with her and squeezed her hand. "Promise you'll let me know where you are at all times? Maybe you could wear a watch or something that allows me to keep track of where you are, just in case you lose your phone or it runs out of juice."

She squeezed back. "Yeah, I can do that."

Daddio let out a long sigh, closed his eyes for a moment, took a breath, and started the car again. He gave his daughter a warm look before pulling back out onto the highway. They were just a few minutes from home; Jett enjoyed hypnotic glances of sunset sparkling off waving water as they finished the drive.

As he drove his car the final block, Daddio swallowed hard and asked one more question. "What about your emotional health? If I can arrange it, will you see Dr. W more than once a week? Maybe, like, every other day and keep him on call until we have a handle on this?"

"So long as it doesn't cut into my class time, but yeah, I have a lot to catch him up on and I'm thinking we'll need those regular 50-minute check-ins. It's a great idea. Thank you." She plucked at the watch on her wrist as they pulled into the garage. "I'll wear my watch in tracking mode. Anything else?"

He answered as he stepped out of the car. "Yeah, Bug. Don't tell your mom."

Arms folded against her chest, Kathy leaned against the doorframe, barring the space from the garage into the house. "Don't tell me what, Joe?"

Joe jumped. "Oh! Hi Kat. Um, Jett and I were just talking about…" He paused, fumbling for an answer.

Jett laughed internally. Daddio was never any good at lying. Neither was she. She wondered if she got that from him. Still, she tried to rescue him. "About your birthday!"

Kathy pursed her lips. "Mmm-hm. Really?"

Jett nodded, fingers crossed down low and, hopefully, out of sight.

Unsatisfied, Kathy narrowed her eyes at both of them. "My birthday is seven months away," she said frostily. "Now, what were you two really scheming?"

Jett looked at her dad. His turn. She watched his shoulders slump before he caught himself and straightened.

"Well, Kath, Jett and I were just discussing her health," he said, returning her glare. "We've made a temporary plan for extra support while she goes through some things. We've looked at three aspects: physical, emotional, and intellectual. So, I think I've got this one pretty well covered."

He dropped the glare and turned it into a grin. "You taught me well! Are you proud of me for taking a page from the old Kathy book on therapeutic parenting? I got this one!"

Jett smiled. She hoped Mother took this for the truth that it was and didn't push for more details.

"Okay," her mom responded, still frosty. "And how long do you expect me to sit by and watch before I ask more questions? How long do you want me to just observe as you parent without my input?" She was staring Joe down defiantly.

Jett was uncomfortable. She wondered if she could just leave, just walk through the doorway that Mother was blocking. She didn't want to be a part of this conversation, not even as a bystander.

"Hey, Mom? Dad? It's pretty late and I need to get some work done. Is it okay if I just—go up to my room for a bit?"

Kathy's expression softened infinitesimally. "Sure, Jett. Let me know if you need any help. I'll be in the kitchen getting dinner served. Plan to be ready to eat in about 15 minutes, okay?"

Jett scooted by her mom. "Yeah, okay. Thanks." She looked back and gave Daddio an apologetic shrug from behind Mother's back. "Thanks for the ride home," she said. "It was fun hanging out with you."

Jett ran up the stairs, going over the plan in her mind. What would help her find Sam? But, wait. She needed to be clear on what she had committed to. Physical safety: stay with people who knew her dad's number in case she blacked out or something. Emotional safety: talk to Dr. W more often. Intellectual safety: only with those first two in place could she then follow the clues to sort out the mystery of Sam. Yes. She could do all that.

Now in her room, Jett looked at her boards. She had one for the dog, one for Sam, and one for Ruby. She started new ones for Andy and Carlos. Jett had notes to add, not just to the new boards, but to all of them. After all, each of the other members of the Core5 needed to seek some kind of safety. They could use this for their project. And the dog? That seemed like the only unrelated board. Jett herself didn't have a board because she wasn't in danger. Or was she? Could the dog help with that? Hmmm. So many things to consider.

Picking up a stack of sticky notes, Jett got to work. She had clues to note, threads to follow. Her night was just beginning.

18

ARRIVING AT DR. W's office, Jett fell into her favorite overstuffed chair there. Another weekend approached and her thoughts raced in overdrive. She'd spent another late night looking for clues to puzzles she couldn't solve. How could she best use her campus free time to protect her Core5, find Sam, and get the final project for their sophomore year into shape?

She kept getting sidetracked and hadn't texted Ruby yet. Would this weekend be the right time? Not many weeks of the school year remained. Then it would be summer. Summer! What would happen *then*? That unwieldy open schedule gaped at her like the jaws of a shark, unhinged and ready to swallow her whole.

She gulped and looked up. "Dr. W? May I ask you a question?"

Dr. W smiled at Jett's initial query. This question had become part of their ritual greeting and he leaned forward eagerly, waiting. He peered into her like he wanted to find out what came next.

"Sure, Jett. Go ahead. What's on your mind?"

"Well, a lot of things, actually." Couldn't he see the ocean of thoughts waiting to carry her away if she wasn't careful? Jett studied his expression and nodded to herself. No, apparently he couldn't.

Dr. W continued to smile and nod at her as he crossed his legs at the ankles and leaned back in his chair. His hands rested, fingers interlaced, folded in his lap.

Thinking Dr. W looked like a regal figure from a storybook or maybe a movie, she tilted her head into the silence. It was time to share her thoughts.

"First of all, I want to understand the boundaries here," she said with a tentative note in her voice. "What can I tell you in confidence? What are you mandated to report? And how do I sort out if I'm crossing any of those lines?"

Dr. W suddenly sat up straight again. He spoke with measured tones. "Jett, to this day, you never cease to surprise or amaze me. Today you surprised me and I must admit I'm a bit concerned. How about you tell me what's happening and I'll tell you if it's something I need to report."

Jett thought he might even be holding his breath as he awaited her response. She regretted having to disappoint him. "Um, sorry Doc, but that won't work," she said with a slow shake of her head. "These things aren't mine to tell. If I'm going to share them anyway, then I need to know up front what I can tell you without it going beyond being our private conversation."

Even though it was excruciatingly uncomfortable for her, Jett stared directly into his eyes, hoping he could feel her sincerity and determination. She would protect her friends, no matter what. She just needed some help sorting out how to do that. Breaking her eye contact, Dr. W slowly stood and methodically paced. Eyes squinting and hands knotted tightly behind his back, he frowned. Dr. W stared off into the distance, looking at something she couldn't see. He bowed his head. His voice was low when he finally responded.

"Okay. That's fair. Here's how I see it," he began. "It's my role at Presidio Prep to help our students navigate their time here, both on campus and off. I enjoy focusing on the issues brought to me by students because usually they bring me interesting but relatively easy puzzles."

That startled Jett. She had never brought him a puzzle. Was she supposed to bring him a puzzle?

He continued without seeming to notice her surprise. "You, however, keep me engaged by challenging my brain and filling my heart with hope. I know no other 15-year-old who thinks so deeply, so strategically, as you do. I don't know who's in trouble or what we're facing, but I want to help. If they aren't students here, I'll only be able to help you, since you fall under my jurisdiction. But if whoever you are concerned about also goes here, I can get involved.

I'm assuming they are students here, maybe even part of your Core5."

Jett nodded slowly, affirming his conclusion. How had he figured that out? Did he know all of her friends were in danger?

"Here's the technicality, then. If they are *a* danger to themselves or to others, I am compelled to report it. However, if they are *in* danger, I will consult you, but I feel strongly compelled to get them the support they need. I'm hopeful that, between the two of us, we can resolve the issue. Does this make sense?"

Jett nodded mutely again. *In* danger—that meant she could tell him. Right?

He paused and fixed her with an intense look. "Will you tell me more now? This sounds like something you shouldn't have to carry on your own." He locked eyes with her just as her face relaxed into a relieved smile.

Jett turned around to her spiky backpack and opened it to reveal a set of foam core boards. "I can do you one better, Doc. I'll show you." On top of his organized desk, she laid the boards out, one by one, so they could both see all of them. There were four boards, one for each of her four team members, all labeled with their names.

Jett watched Dr. W's mouth drop open as he took in her work. His reaction reminded Jett of her neighbor, Ben, whom she used to see daily. With a sharp pang alerting her heart, she realized that she hadn't seen Ben lately; she wondered if he had moved or whether Yoda's absence was somehow behind their separation. She missed his patience, insights, and kindness.

"I don't know what to say."

Jett felt his eyes on her, and she looked down, retreating into her work. "Why, Doc? They're just boards. I have bigger ones, more complex ones, at home, but I thought this might help us."

Dr. W let out a low chortle of awe. "Jett, I think these should be called your brilliant boards."

From under her lashes, she peeked at him. Was he making fun of her? What was the big deal?

"Really!" he emphasized, running his hands along the edges of a board. "These show how your mind works around a hypothesis and through a problem. Besides the obvious—that you have a board for each member of your team—can you tell me what they have in common? Why did you make them?"

"There's a board for each person because each one is in danger and I don't know how to help them," she said carefully, willing him to see it as she did. "I'm not even sure how to prioritize who needs me most and who would be better off without intervention."

She paused to ensure he got it and watched him carefully inspect each one. Jett thought she heard him kind of stutter under his breath.

"Each one is in… oh. *Oh!* My. Okay. Yes. I see…" Dr. W looked at her. "You know some of these you can't solve, right? Maybe even all of them. But we *can* work on them. Every one of them, in fact." She noticed how his hands touched each board with reverence. "Jett, which one are you most concerned about?"

At that, she took a deep breath and jumped in. She told him everything. About Sam going missing. About Ruby being whisked away and asking for texts. She told him about being with Carlos and Andy in public when they were doing nothing wrong and yet were thrown on concrete by the police. "My dad says it was because they're teenage boys with a skin color other than white." She looked at him standing stock-still, a regal man who had probably lived it, listening to her explain her first experience of racism.

"Do you think that was the first time Carlos or Andy had been misjudged because of the color of their skin?" He tilted his head as if it would help him hear her answer.

Jett's eyes grew round and her mouth parted. "I…" She furrowed her brow and bit her lip anxiously as she reached up with her hand and began pinching her own neck. She felt herself slipping deep into her thoughts. "I don't know. It never occurred to me. I didn't even know there was such a thing." She looked Dr. W in the eyes as her hand slowly stilled. Jett swallowed the tightness in her throat. "We can't solve this one, can we? It's something I'm just going to have to keep working on, isn't it?"

Dr. W nodded slowly. "It's one we're *all* going to have to keep working on." He set aside the boys' boards and picked up a different one. "Is Ruby safe?"

Jett nodded briefly, then switched to shaking her head. "She is, yes. But also no," she said. "She's safe because she's in hiding somewhere and her parents have lots of money, so they can hire people to look out for her. But she's still in danger because there are men who her family consider creepy—people she doesn't know—looking for her." Jett paused again, considering. "Maybe they wouldn't be looking for her if they knew how mean her friends are. Seriously. She spends time with some pretty rotten people."

Dr. W smiled sadly. "I'm afraid it doesn't work like that, Jett," he said. "A stalker means she is in danger because someone is obsessing about her and won't allow her any privacy. They are harassing and maybe even threatening her. That's pretty serious stuff. A group of mean girls won't keep them away from her. There are things she can do to protect herself, and it sounds like her family has it all under control for now. But safety *will* be an ongoing issue for her, just as it is for any high-profile person."

Jett took mental notes mutely about the additional Post-Its she'd have to put on the boards at home. Then she reached out to touch Sam's board. "Which brings us to Sam." She fixed pleading eyes on him. "We have to find her."

"Yes, we do. Absolutely," Dr. W agreed. "And I would like to bring in a team to do exactly that."

Jett's heart plummeted as she shook her head vigorously at him. Gut instinct told her Sam would be furious at this betrayal and may choose to hide or run away in response. She backed away from Dr. W. Had she said too much?

"Jett, hear me out. This may be serious and I believe we need all the help we can get to find her quickly. She's been gone not only from school but from Grams for—what? A week? A month? Longer? The longer we wait, the worse it's going to get."

"But, Doc, *we* can find her! She sings at the Montgomery BART station and on the trains." Jett clapped a hand over her mouth. She hadn't meant to tell him. It wasn't hers to share. She watched as his eyebrows rose. He looked baffled.

"Does she now? And you think we can find her there? Would you recognize her voice?"

Jett stepped back up to his desk as she nodded. She rose to the balls of her feet, rocking up and down in excitement. "She does. I do. Yes. I will. I know it."

Her enthusiasm mollified him just enough to win a brief concession. With a quick nod, he outlined his idea. "Sounds like we need an emergency field trip for your team as soon as possible. I will wait to bring others in until after we try. *Once*," he emphasized. "But after that first try, that's it. I *must* expand the team. Right away. I know that's not what you want to hear, but we need to get moving on this to protect Sam. I'll arrange it on my end. Can you get the boys on board?"

"Of course."

Suddenly, he looked older to Jett, but she shrugged that off and sighed in relief as her rocking slowed to a stop. They were making a plan. Dr. W would help. They would find Sam.

19

AS SHE REVIEWED the events of the past week, Jett struggled to stay awake. Depression and overwhelm held her down like a weighted blanket. For some reason, she had expected more. Maybe it was getting help from another adult besides Daddio, maybe it was her desperation, and maybe—just maybe—it was having been *so close* to finding Sam at the BART on her own that one time, but by now, she had expected Sam to be an active part of the Core5 again. Jett was wrong. So now what? Sam was still out there somewhere. Wasn't she? She just *had* to be. Jett would *not* entertain any other option.

Bone weary, she finally lay down, still actively worrying. What should she do *now*? Dr. W had reported Sam as missing after their last failed attempt to find her. That created an official case and a file number. Jett had added it to her Sam board. She knew police were out searching, but no one knew Sam like she did. She believed the kinds of details only she could provide could make or break the case. Jett knew so many things she thought she should share—and yet she knew nothing at all. How would she... Mercifully at last, Jett fell asleep, fixated on the questions, clues, and tangents that repeatedly assaulted her mind.

In the middle of the night, a phone rang. She heard it. Or thought she did. She wasn't sure. Was a phone really—Yep. There it was again. Groggily, she peered at the screen but didn't recognize the number. She thought about it. Should she answer? Who called at this hour?

Jett answered tentatively. "Hello?"

Deep bass tones thumped through the earpiece. And laughter. She recognized laughter. Who was up listening to music, laughing, and calling her at—she glanced at her bedside clock—1:52 in the morning?

A muffled voice barely came through, as if the person calling held their hand over the mouthpiece. "Jett?"

Jett's breath caught in her throat even as her heartbeat raced. They knew her! Whoever called had *meant* to call *her*. "Yes, this is Jett Harper. May I help you?"

She heard a long, quavering sigh. "Oh, gawd. Oh, Jett." And then just uncontrolled *whimpering? Crying?* What was going on?

As she struggled to make sense of the sounds, Jett wondered which of her boards would later hold the details of this plot twist. She listened intently. Who was crying while everyone else was laughing? A choked sob froze her spinning thoughts.

The voice was muffled, but the message wasn't. "Jett? Is it really you? You said if I'd be yours, you'd also be my everywhere friend. Well, I'm still yours. Are you still mine? If so, you're my only one. Will you come help me? Please. I need you." Now the crying was punctuated by ragged breathing.

The sounds finally cleared the fog from her brain. She sat up straight in her bed and forgot about whispering, despite the hour. "Sam? *Sam?* Where are you? What's happening? Of course I'm your everywhere friend! You're my *best* friend. Where are you? I'll come now. I can pull up a ride on my app or ask Daddio to drive me." She got out of bed, propped the phone against her shoulder, and started grabbing clothes to put on. She heard a sharp intake of breath and a muttered curse. It was closer than the laughter, closer than the music. She thought it was Sam, but she wasn't sure.

Jett overheard someone coming close, or at least, she thought that was what she heard. Sam had stopped talking and seemed to be turned away from the phone. Afraid to hang up, afraid to lose Sam again, Jett's knuckles turned white as she clutched her phone. She listened closely. Sam's breath was loud but steady. Someone was definitely asking her a question. She strained to hear Sam's response. Her voice sounded funny.

"Hey, Jake. Yeah, I have your phone," she said in a faux casual tone. "I needed to call my girl. She'd love it here. Your place is dope. You don't mind me inviting her over, do you? She's fine. She's white sugar. She's pure snow. Let me see if I can talk her into coming over to meet you."

Jett knew it was rude to eavesdrop, but she felt compelled to do it. Mother would be so disappointed. Good thing she was out of town. Jett had never heard this tone in Sam's voice before. She was curious and a little—okay, a *lot*—concerned. What was going on? What was Sam talking about? Who was this Jake? Why did Sam call her "sugar" and "snow"? None of this made any sense. She barely breathed as she waited for answers.

She heard movement, muffled sounds that almost seemed like moans of pain. Was Sam hurt?

Sam's tone changed again. "Okay, J. I'll be there in a minute. Let me just wrap this up."

Jett heard a low male chuckle and maybe a door closing. *Was* that a door closing? Jett thought she might be getting better at this, but it was so hard to be certain of anything over the phone.

"Dorothy? You there?"

Jett answered right away. "Yes, I'm here. I'm dressed and ready to go. I can come to that… that, Jake, is it? Is that what you want?"

"NO!" Sam practically shouted, then she sighed. "No. Just no. I had to say that, but you can't come here. Meet me. I'll find a way to slip out of here and hope he doesn't notice." Jett could barely hear Sam, but she thought she might be talking to herself anyway. "I think I can get away with that. I'll just say I'm waiting on the porch and then I'll start walking. Yeah, that should work."

"Where are you? Where *exactly*, I mean…"

Sam was silent for a moment. "I'm in San Francisco somewhere. There are a lot of trees. I think they're cypress. And maybe eucalyptus. There's also a roundabout. It's white and has a fountain. And I can see the ocean. Lots of big old homes. Do you know where I'm talking about? I'll have to leave his phone behind or he'll find me. I also need to figure out how to erase your number." Panic bled through the line. "Oh, Jett. Maybe this is a bad idea. I shouldn't get you involved. But I don't know what else to do! Help me—I mean, can you? What do we do?" Sam's voice had dropped so low Jett could barely hear her. Jett was pacing in circles with the phone jammed hard against her ear when she heard the crying start up again.

Her protective instinct took over and she put her phone on speaker. "Sam, just breathe for a minute. And stay on the phone. Stay with me! Do you understand? I've got you. We've got this. My Daddio is going to bring me there. I think you're talking about St. Francis Wood. He grew up there. Go to the fountain as soon as it's safe. Stay in the shadows until you see us. We're coming. Don't worry about Jake having my number. Daddio will know how to fix it. Just stay safe. We will find you. Can you do that?"

She turned to find Daddio in her doorway, keys in hand, dressed in his sweats. He didn't question. He didn't blink. Daddio nodded to her and gently took the phone from her hand as they started down the hall.

"Sam, can you hear me? This is Jett's dad, Joe." He spoke soothingly, but with authority. "I'm so glad you called. We're on our way. Can you stay on the phone for a while longer? Or do you need to go? It's important you find the right time to sneak away. Listen to me. Do whatever keeps you safe."

Sam sounded like she was pulling herself together, gathering courage from his strength. "Hi, Mr. Harper. I'm so sorry to bother you," she said, controlling her voice now. "Jett's my only everywhere friend and I didn't know who else to call. This is not how I wanted to meet you." She barked out a short, humorless laugh. "I'm going to go rejoin the party so I can look for a chance to slip out. I'll be by the fountain as soon as I can. *Please* come fast."

As they got in the car, Joe set the phone on the dash, punched the garage door opener, and started up the engine. "We're on our way, Sam. It's going to be okay. Just stay safe. *Get* safe."

Jett grabbed the phone as she heard the disconnecting beep. She held on tight, as the car roared out of the neighborhood and raced toward the Golden Gate Bridge on its way to the place her Daddio had grown up, just like his Daddio before him. Small world. Sam was near the place her great-grandparents had settled. A torrent of things was happening inside her body. She wasn't sure what she felt. Everything was jumbled—fear, excitement, anxiety, awe. Soon, Jett would see Sam.

They were on their way.

20

JETT STRAINED TO see out the car window. Usually, she savored crossing the Golden Gate Bridge, passing through the Presidio, and buzzing up 19th Avenue. Now, looking forward onto Santa Clara Avenue, Jett stared at the burbling fountain. She willed Sam to be there, to appear. And yet, she did not.

Turning her pleading eyes onto Daddio, she knew he could fix this. He would find Sam. Jett felt awkward trying to think of new words when Princess Leia had said it so clearly for her. So she whispered the shared truth: "You're my only hope." It's how she felt. Daddio was the only one who could put the pieces together. Her system was overloading with both hopefulness and helplessness. Where was Sam?

A uniformed private security guard stood near the spot where she had expected to see Sam. He was talking to someone, but she couldn't see who. What was he saying?

Jett wished she could read lips. Maybe that could be her focus for the summer, a tool to make life easier. She made a mental note: Become a lip reader.

Daddio pulled into an open parking spot, turned the car's engine off, and sat quietly for a moment. Hands in his lap, he looked like he was thinking. Slowly, he turned toward his watching daughter. He took an exaggerated breath, gulping in the heady mix of eucalyptus and ocean. He gave Jett a slight nod, then watched and waited for her to take a deep breath, too. She did.

"You ready, kiddo?"

"Are you, Daddio?"

They nodded in unison. "Okay then," Joe said. "Let's go get our girl."

Jett stepped out first. Loose gravel under her Keds sounded so loud to her ears, and she slipped a little before regaining her footing. The security guard turned toward the sound of their arrival. Immediately, she saw what he had unintentionally been blocking from view, and Jett lurched forward.

"Sam!"

Sam quickly put a finger to her lips, but couldn't hide her delight at seeing Jett. "Shush, you! Stealth mode, remember?"

Tears streaking down her face but still smiling, Jett had a fleeting thought that this must be what crazy looked like. She didn't care. Sam was here.

As Jett enfolded her friend in her arms, she felt the chill of Sam's skin and realized that the skimpy outfit she wore exposed entirely too much of that skin.

Unwilling to let Sam go just yet, she called over her shoulder. "Daddio, I need a coat or something warm. Can you please bring me something warm?"

Jett heard him rummaging in the car as she continued to savor the reunion. He must have found something, because suddenly he was there, arms stretched wide with a blanket. He wrapped it around both girls.

The security guard eyed them cautiously. "So, this girl belongs to you?" he asked Joe. "She looks too young to be out here alone. And dressed like *that*? I don't need to tell *you* that not everyone would take her age into account when seeing such a body on display like—"

"Agreed," Joe cut in. "It's why we're here to take her home. Thank you for keeping an eye on her while you were on patrol. Tell the Harpers over on San Anselmo Avenue that their boyo and grandy stopped by and you helped them out. Tell them we had to go but will visit soon. Will you? I bet my mum will have a nice sweet treat in exchange for this news."

"Ah! Mr. Harper, is it?" The guard relaxed immediately as he brightened up. "You must be the famous Joe. I know your parents. They're good folks. Of course, I'll let them know, with or without a reward from your mum's kitchen. But I must admit I've heard tales of her legendary sweets. Thank you!"

"Sure thing. Now let me get these two into the car."

Just then, they heard the distress call come over the guard's walkie-talkie. Apparently, he was supposed to be on the lookout for a beautiful young black girl who disappeared from a party a few blocks away. The dispatch said the girl was on medications and could be delusional. If anyone found her, they were to return her to the house, whatever story she concocted.

The guard studied Joe, who held both girls protectively in his arms. "Go now. Quickly," he said softly but firmly. "I don't like this one bit. I'm not paid to be party to whatever is going on there, but I ain't gonna lie and tell you I'll stand up to them. Right now, I've got to go lie myself into a free conscience. I ain't seen nothin'. Met no one. So—go. Get safe. And be careful." He looked directly at Sam. "Don't come back."

Sam ducked her head and muttered "yes" as she and Jett raced back to Daddio's car. Jett held the back door open for Sam to jump in, the blanket still wrapped around her, and then launched herself into the front seat. Joe pulled smoothly back onto Santa Clara Avenue and accelerated out of the neighborhood. As they approached 19th, all three of them let out a collective sigh of relief.

Jett was the first to break the silence. "Sam? Where are your clothes?"

Daddio and Sam burst out laughing. Jett didn't. How was that funny?

"I actually don't know, Dorothy," Sam said. "Maybe the Tin Man has them?"

Jett could hear the forced smile in Sam's reply and accepted her response mutely. Clothes, or the lack thereof, wasn't the real question anyway. New clothes were easy to acquire. The next questions would be harder. Jett tried to come up with what Dr. W would ask, but she just didn't know. The only thing she *did* know was that Sam probably needed to sing, just like that first time Jett heard her in the music hall. In any event, she certainly needed to hear Sam's song. Maybe that would help her know the next question.

"Daddio? I think we need to make a stop. Would that be okay?" Jett glanced back at Sam, who shrugged, then at Daddio, who made a surprised face but didn't refuse.

"Okay, kiddo. What're you thinking? Anywhere specific in mind? Maybe food? I don't know where to take us, though."

"No, Daddio. I know you won't understand this, but if you have gym clothes Sam can borrow—"

"Yep! And they're even clean!"

Jett snorted softly at how proud Daddio was about that. "Okay, well—I want to stop off at Baker's Beach." She turned to Sam. "Sam, will you bundle up in Daddio's super-soft workout wear and go to the beach with me for just a bit? I don't know if *you* need this, but *I* do."

Sam was staring at her, her mouth in a tight, straight line. Jett felt the awkward weight of her discomfort. How should she navigate this moment? What was she supposed to do? She decided to put her thoughts out there.

"Will you sing like you did that very first time I heard you?" she asked tentatively. "That's when I learned about the magic of music. Can you do that for me again now? Please?"

When Jett turned all the way around to look at Sam, she saw tears silently running down her face. It looked like Sam was shaking as she swallowed heavily, her chest heaving. Wordlessly, Sam nodded and looked down at her lap, the one covered by the soft warm blanket Daddio had wrapped around them both. Finally, she raised her head and locked eyes with Jett, who was still carefully cataloging her reactions.

"Okay, Daddio," Jett said, swiveling back around to address Joe. "If you're willing, it's settled. Sam needs to sing and I need to hear it. Baker's Beach?"

"Sure thing," he agreed. "But just so you know, I'm coming, too. It's very late and dark. I promise I won't interfere, but I need to keep an eye on you both. That's the deal."

Sam cried harder.

At the beach parking lot, Sam layered on the clothes from Daddio's gym bag. The trio held hands as they walked across the sand toward the water's edge.

Jett let go first, freeing Sam to approach the water. Daddio hung back. Jett stood a few steps behind, but she could hear Sam's clear, mesmerizing tone as it seared the skies and met the ocean. Her music had its own power, its own rolling vibration of anger, of sadness, of confusion and clarity. This was not a song Jett knew, and she wondered if it was one anyone had heard before. The emotions she felt witnessing Sam's song were another bit of magic. Her heart swelled as she realized how much she had missed this.

The song turned into keening. Jett knew this was the beginning of a new song, one that Sam had taught her, so she stepped up and joined in. She stood side by side with her idol, her friend, her—her *Sam*. And as they wove their songs together, she could feel the healing. This time, Sam reached over for her. Jett knew then that she would, in time, hear from Sam all she needed to know and all that Sam needed to share. As their song concluded, they turned together back to Daddio.

He was waiting on the sand, watching them approach. Daddio started to speak. Stopped. Shook his head and began again. A sigh escaped as he reached out his arms, offering a hug to both girls. They walked into his arms.

"I don't know what to say. I am… honored? I am shaken. And I am moved. And… and I—" His voice choked off as both girls burrowed deeper into his protective embrace.

"Shhh. It's okay," she crooned to him, patting his arm, as she had once seen Miya do with Sam. "I know exactly what you're going through. I did, too, the first time I heard Sam sing. Just allow yourself to feel it. We'll talk later."

And so they stood there, feeling it, together. They held onto each other until the hope overrode the hurt. They held on until it was time to move forward and then they did—together.

In the car, it was Sam's turn to break the silence. "I'm sorry to cause you so much trouble, Mr. Harper," she began. "I didn't know who else to call. Grams already thinks I'm with you guys and I lied about where I was going because I wanted to surprise her with the best news."

"It's okay, Sam," Joe assured her. "I mean, it's *not*, but I'm so glad you're safe. From what I understand, though, you've been gone quite a while. I know Jett has been worried sick about you. Can you tell us more? Or do you want to wait until we get home? You *are* coming home with us, right? My wife is away, so it's just me and the Lovebug, but we hope you'll agree to stay over. Okay?" He paused and then added, "I make a mean grilled cheese." He was grinning.

Sam smiled right back at him. Jett could hear it in her reply. "You had me at grilled cheese."

She watched Daddio's shoulders drop in relief as they crossed onto the Golden Gate Bridge. Soon they would be safe at home. There would be time enough to learn Sam's story.

21

STANDING IN FRONT of Presidio Prep after the four-day weekend, Jett let out a sigh. She had mixed emotions about being back here already. Sam's call and stealth extraction had been on Thursday night. Could it really be Monday? She had enjoyed having Sam practically to herself—with Daddio, of course, who had taken to Sam just as Jett knew he would. He was such a good Daddio. Jett tuned back into what he and Sam were talking about right in front of her.

"Seriously, Mr. H, I promise. I've learned my lesson. You keep saying you've never heard a voice like mine and that's awesome. *Really,*" Sam said patiently. "You've been saying it all weekend. But you gotta know that my voice is what got me into this trouble in the first place. You're just gonna have to believe me. I'll be okay."

With Daddio's attention focused on Sam, Jett took the opportunity to study him. He seemed unusually tired. Didn't he sleep at all this weekend? "Daddio? Are you okay?"

"Yeah, kiddo," he said, turning his attention to her. He pinched the bridge of his nose briefly. "I'm just—" He shook his head to clear it and then pinned Sam to the spot with his eyes. Sam froze in place.

"Okay, Sam, here's the deal," he said, switching to lawyer mode. "I'm not gonna push you. That's not how you'll learn to trust me. But I will be here for you, just like I am for Jett. So—here's your phone." Daddio handed Sam a brand new way to connect with the world.

"Are you *for real?* Mr. H, I—" Sam looked down at the phone but didn't reach for it.

Joe pushed it closer, insisting. "I know my Bug told you I'm stubborn and hard-headed and that I fight like a lawyer. Believe her. Take the phone and our contract will be considered valid. Here are the terms: You will answer when I call or text—every time, with candid truth. In return, I will answer when you call or text unless I'm in court. And if I am in court, someone will answer for me. I'll call you back as soon as I can."

Resigned, but smiling slightly, Sam accepted the phone.

"Okay. Anything else?"

"Yes," he said, still staring her down. "I'll be calling your Grams or stopping by to see her—*today*. Not to rat you out, but to tell her just how much we enjoy having you stay and that she's doing me a favor by allowing Jett to have so much time with such a good friend. I want her to know you're invited to stay with us on weekends and weeknights or whatever suits you and Jett, especially with this big project looming."

He relaxed the intensity of his look, but didn't let her off the hook just yet. "Will that work for you? Will you allow us to be another home base?"

Sam, looking like she might cry, swallowed hard before launching herself at Daddio and throwing her arms around his neck.

It startled Jett. Here they were in the middle of campus, where anyone could see them, but Sam didn't mind being affectionate with Daddio, even in public. According to her research, developmentally at this age and stage, she and Sam were supposed to shy away from connection to adults. But, once again, Sam defied the rules. Jett was glad. It gave her permission to do the same, and she launched herself at them both. Jett could hear both tears and a broad smile in Daddio's tone.

"All right, all right! I'll take that as a yes. Now scoot, you two. I called Dr. W and he's expecting you both right about now." As they released him, he turned his attention back to Sam. "He's someone I've come to trust. I know Jett speaks with him regularly. Will you do that, too? Confide in him?"

Jett nodded eagerly. "I like talking to him. I feel like he gets it. He's on my side."

"He is, kiddo," Daddio said. "And I know he'll be on yours, too, Sammy."

Sammy? Not Sam? Jett thought it interesting that Daddio had given Sam a nickname of sorts. Did anyone else call her Sammy? Sam didn't seem to mind.

Pausing in front of the administration wing, Joe looked at Sam. "Do you know what the traditional meaning of your name is?" She shook her head slightly, perplexed. "It means 'God heard.'" He and Jett both smiled broadly. "Well, we did, too. Now let the doc hear, okay?" He shooed them forward with a quick gesture of his hands.

They walked into the building together, Jett working hard to contain her excitement but still bouncing and Sam looking thoughtful. In front of the door to Dr. Williams' office, she took a deep and measured breath in through her nose. Jett followed suit, took her hand, and they walked in together.

Jett felt so excited she thought she might burst. "Hi, Dr. W! Do you remember my friend Sam? She's back! And we need to get her caught up. I want—"

Dr. W held up a hand, interrupting Jett's effusive greeting. "Hi, Jett. Hold on a minute. Let's back up. We don't know what Sam wants."

He bowed his head at Sam and grinned. "Hi, Sam. Nice to see you again. It's been a while. Do you want to ease into this with small talk or do you already know what you want?"

Jett smirked. Small talk? That definitely would not be an effective use of time. Folding her arms across her chest, she rocked back on her heels and waited. She was trying so hard to be patient. But if someone didn't speak soon, she would…

"Hey there, Doc," Sam said, stealing a glance at Jett. "I don't know you like Jett does. In fact, I remember the one time we met was because of my friend here. But I trust her. If she says we can talk, then we can talk. Real talk."

She smiled indulgently at Jett. "Besides, I think she'll blow a gasket if we don't get to it soon."

Jett heard Dr. W chuckle as he stepped aside to let them in. Sam would've been right if Jett were a car. But how was this funny? She'd been gone a long time. It was time to find out why.

"Jett, you might want to give me a moment alone with Sam," Dr. W said. "I'm not sure what she's ready to share with us both." He looked quizzically between the two girls.

Jett started forward at this. Was he kicking her out? "Wait! What?"

She looked at Sam, who shrugged her shoulders. Jett's eyes squinted involuntarily as she tried to process this unfathomable possibility. She straightened herself to her full height, squared her shoulders, and set her jaw. She needed to set Dr. W straight.

"I don't think *you* understand. This is my friend, my every-where, every-day, no-matter-what, *best* friend. She can tell me *anything*. Actually, she needs to. How else will I sort out how to be the best best-friend to her?" She glanced at Sam for confirmation. "Right, Sam?"

Sam inclined her head slightly. "Then it's settled," Jett informed Dr. W. "*I'm* staying. *You* can leave, Dr. W, but I'm not going anywhere."

Dr. W's face appeared to light up. He tried valiantly to swallow a laugh. Dr. W ended up gulping loudly before nodding. Jett began to relax, just a little bit. He understood. The two of them focused on Sam, who was watching their interaction with a look Jett could only interpret as surprise.

"Well, Sam, you heard her," Dr. W said, still choking back a laugh. "And I've decided to stay. Are you ready to spill?"

"I... wow!" Sam seemed nonplussed. "Is it always like this?"

It was Doc's turn to shrug. "Kind of. I never know what Jett has up her sleeve."

Jett rolled her eyes at this. Yes, he did—her arm. She started pulling at her neck irritably. Could they please get on with it already? Extra energy from all the waiting was building up steam inside her. Jett saw Sam's eyes dart at her unconscious neck-pulling and, with effort, stopped herself. Things had better get moving soon or—

Sam closed her eyes, took a deep breath, and let it out loudly. "Okay. Here's what's going on—First though, Doc, tell me where you grew up."

He looked briefly taken aback and then smiled at her. "No one here has ever asked," he said. "I grew up relatively near here, in the eastern part of the Bay Area. There's this little town north of Berkeley called Richmond. Where I'm from is referred to as the Iron Triangle. Know it?"

Sam nodded and relaxed a little, as if she'd settled her mind about something. "Okay. Well…" She gave Jett a perplexing look. "I live in Oakland—the *real* Oakland, not the prettified, poster child for urban infusion, but the real, raw, gritty, clawing-your-way-through-life-just-to-survive Oakland."

Dr. W seemed to understand something Sam wasn't saying. Jett squinted again, trying to piece it together and catch up.

This was all new for her. She certainly hadn't heard any of this from Sam. Was this what Sam meant when she talked around being poor? Was she, like, *really* poor? Not just the middle class, need-to-make-a-tighter-budget kind of poor? Jett couldn't process it. After all, Andy lived in Oakland, too.

Jett gave Sam a concerned look. "Kinda like Andy?"

"Nope. Not kinda like Andy."

"Like me," volunteered Dr. W.

Sam seemed to think about this for a moment. "Yeah, Doc. Maybe like you, but also maybe not so much," she said, studying him as she did so. "In my world, you don't break out of it. Families rarely move from our kind to, well, their kind." She gestured at Jett.

It was Jett's turn to be taken aback. Her *kind*? What did Sam actually mean by—

But Dr. W was way ahead of her. "Okay, like me, but before I was here," he said. "Before I clawed my way into scholarships and grants to get out. Sam, I know you can't see it right now, but that's *just like me.*"

Jett kept her eyes riveted on Sam. She didn't want to miss any nuance given away by body language, and Jett thought she saw the moment Sam took Dr. W's meaning in, when she smiled. Still studying her carefully, Jett thought she saw a glimmer of hope light Sam's eyes.

"All right, Doc, maybe like you, but then again, maybe not," she conceded. "It's been just my sister and me since the parentals left, one to jail and one to the grave. My Grams would say to the heavens. She took us in after that. She worked three jobs to feed us and clothe us and keep us. But she's old and one day her body wouldn't let her keep doing it. So, my sister took over some of the money making. She started singing on BART."

Sam stopped and scratched slowly at invisible dirt on her pants. When no one commented, she continued her story.

"I guess she had watched others do it, and she just learned how on her own. She put herself through junior college that way and helped take care of us." Her voice wavered a bit and her eyes misted as she thought back. "She even taught me some. That is, before she went off with the touring cast for a big show."

Sam sounded like she was having a hard time breathing, her lungs filling and emptying with quick and shallow gasps. Jett took an exaggerated breath and held it briefly, willing Sam with her eyes to do the same. She then moved directly in front of Sam and crouched down right in front of her to catch her attention. With her next dramatic breath, Sam burst out laughing.

"Dorothy, I love you," she said, shaking her head in amusement but working to correct her breathing all the same.

Jett dropped her shoulders in relief. She knew Sam meant her and she knew they were going to be all right. They would get through this together. She felt giddy with that knowledge.

"Tell us more, Sam," she urged. "I want to understand."

"Doc, my sister has been gone since the end of summer," she said as she let out a long breath. "And the tour is costing her most of her wages, so she can't send as much back as she expected. I know Grams is picking up shifts. She's trying to make up the difference. But really, it's up to me."

She closed her eyes, hung her head, and furrowed her brow. After two shaky breaths, she opened her eyes and locked her gaze on Jett, who held onto her arm with both hands, trying hard to be supportive.

"So—most of this year I've been singing on the BART trains and in the stations, trying to make up the difference. Sometimes I do, sometimes I don't. There's not enough time in just my commute," she shrugged toward Dr. W, who kept a steady gaze on her but didn't make a sound. "I gotta sing more to make bank. But Grams doesn't know I've been missing school. She'd be *furious*. It was hard for me to get accepted here in the first place and then to figure out how to get here each day, so I didn't tell her. I think Grams sees this place like some kind of way out of our 'hood."

At last, Dr. W broke his silence. "And do *you* see this place as a way out of the cycle you were born into?"

"Well, maybe. But Grams doesn't know how hard it is to do school and make money. I gave up on all the convenience and comfort things a while ago, like eating here on campus, but then I had to give up my cell phone. I figured she wouldn't know. She doesn't call it, and it's just one more bill. Miya used to pay all of those. After she left, I couldn't keep up."

Sam was wringing her hands, but stopped abruptly. Her tone shifted. "That is—until a producer found me. Actually, he's not just a producer. He owns a label and he wanted me to record at his studio. This guy advanced me enough to leave some for Grams and get to his studio here in the City. He said I have a voice like no other he's ever heard," she added, looking ruefully at Jett. "Sound familiar?"

Jett nodded slowly, deciding not to share how much she disliked that someone had stolen Daddio's words.

"I wasn't sure how much I would earn right away and I wanted to surprise Grams, so I told her I'd be with you," she said as she started wringing her hands again. "I'm sorry."

Sam deflated before their eyes.

"Yeah, well, that was all a lie," she continued. "Afterward, he took me to his fancy digs near that place you picked me up. He had a home studio too and a lot of nice stuff, but also a lot of not so nice—umm—stuff."

Sam fell silent, staring at her hands as she continued to work them around and around. "Once I got there, I didn't know what to do," she admitted. "It felt all wrong, but I didn't have my phone anymore, so I borrowed his phone without him knowing and I called Jett." She turned to face Doc. "I didn't know what else to do."

Gently, he put a hand on her shoulder. "You did what you had to, and you made a good choice."

He cleared his throat and turned to Jett. "Jett, I think I need a break. Do you need a break?"

She could feel coils of tension tightening around the air in her body. "I do," she acknowledged. "But I'm also worried about what happens next."

Dr. W put his other hand on Jett's shoulder. "I'll bet. Maybe both of you are. But for now, let's just take a moment and be glad Sam's here. She's safe—for now."

Abruptly, Jett had an inspiration.

"Sam, can you sing?"

Sam stared at her silently.

"Seriously. He should hear you. Everyone should," she said, feeling certain that Sam's music would help somehow. "Will you sing something? Maybe that Dorothy song?"

Sam started nodding slightly. "All right. But it's your song now, so I'm gonna need you to join in, 'k?"

"'K!" Jett replied eagerly.

As Dr. W first experienced the magical tapestry of Sam's music, Jett listened carefully for her cue and soon joined Sam. By the end of the song, Doc was wiping tears from his eyes.

"Girls, I—" he tilted his head and closed his eyes. "I'm going to need a moment. That was a religious experience."

Sam and Jett looked at each other and grinned. Then they waited.

When Dr. Williams finally opened his eyes, he seemed like a man on a mission. "Look, Sam, I *see* you. I need you to know I've got you. We—all three of us—are a team now. I don't have a solution yet for how to keep you in class or make up for the time you lost, but I'll work on it from my end. You two put your heads together and come up with a plan. But don't *do* anything until we've talked about it first. Okay? We need to do better."

He pinned Sam with his eyes. "No more producers unless I vet them," he said, giving her shoulder a closing squeeze before dropping his hand. "In the meantime, come up with options. Brainstorm. Tell me about what you come up with, no matter how crazy. And no more absences. We will make this happen, but *you* need to be here. Promise me you'll show up if I promise to help clear the way."

Sam nodded solemnly at him. Jett, ever the observer, imitated her. Good. It was time for class anyway. Jett understood that Sam wasn't really out of danger yet. Safety was still an issue, just as it was for every other member of their team. But this one, they might be able to affect. Time for a new phase of the plan. Operation Save Sam—continued.

22

THAT AFTERNOON, SAM was taking BART home to Grams, oblivious to the work Jett planned to accomplish.

Jett was on a mission, and as she walked into the Campus Café, her eyes scanned every table and each person in line, searching for Andy and Carlos. As it often did at an inconvenient time, her mind wandered to texting Ruby. One of these days she would just have to stop and message the Princess, both to keep her word but also to ensure Ruby felt part of the group. Then again, she knew Ruby was dealing with bigger issues than feeling like part of the Core5, otherwise she'd be here. Daddio had tried to explain the real dangers stalkers posed for celebrities and public figures but it was beyond Jett's comprehension.

Wait! She heard them. Jett followed the sound, paused in front of Carlos and Andy, and listened. How long had they been here waiting? Had they really moved on from Sam's return and onto soccer?

"That last strike was truly epic! It was straight at the back of the net! Who knew you were actually talented at this?" Andy enthused.

Carlos guffawed. "'Migo! Was this your first time seeing me in action? You haven't been following our season!" He shoved Andy gently on the shoulder. "I'm El Capitán for a reason!" He crossed his arms and lifted his chin with a snort.

Jett thought Carlos really looked perturbed with Andy but considering how important her mission was, she jumped into the conversation *fast* while she still could.

"Hey! Did you even notice Sam at school today?" She pulled on the strap of her trusty armored backpack, the ever-present Spiketus Rex.

"Hey, Manita! Of course I did. I wasn't sure what to say, though. Did you get details out of her? How are we supposed to act now?"

"Are we here to talk about our project? You didn't say, but if so, shouldn't Sam be here too?" asked Andy.

"That's not it," said Jett. "We need to take care of Sam, so I didn't invite her to this meeting. This is about us and what we can do."

Carlos jumped in. "Yeah. And while we were waiting, Andy here was just marvelling at my legendary moves. Have you been to one of my games? I don't remember seeing you."

Jett was baffled. "Me? You want *me* at your game?" This was mystifying. She'd never even considered going to a soccer match. That's what it was called, right? A match? She couldn't imagine why she might want to go.

Carlos appeared just as shocked as she felt. "Of course I *need* you there! I want to hear you cheering me on as I score goal after goal and set up my teammates to do the same. Will you come, 'Manita? Must I beg?" Carlos went to his knees in front of her, hands clasped to his chest, gazing up at Jett and blinking rapidly. Were these the "puppy dog eyes" that she'd heard about? "'Manita, please! Please come to my next game. Please-oh-please!" He flapped a hand up at Andy, urging him forward. "Help me, bro. She's missing out!"

Andy's eyes sparkled with mischief. Jett realized he must be up to something.

"We could go together, Jett!" he said enthusiastically, giving her his most winning smile. "I think they have things you would like at the snack bar and we could pretend to watch Carlos."

Carlos jumped back to his feet and rounded on Andy. "Hey!"

Jett laughed and pretended to push the boys away from each other before she sat down between them. "Okay! Fine! We'll go see Carlos play soccer. But we need to get down to business right now."

Carlos immediately turned serious. "Your text had me worried when you said we needed the whole afternoon and into the evening," he said. "You know all our parents are going to the PTA meeting tonight, right? I already promised I would go. So we need to finish whatever this is before that. Where's Sam? Should we maybe let Ruby know?"

Jett pushed both her palms at him, trying to get him to take a breath. "This is a project we need to nail today for tonight's PTA meeting," she said. "Daddio already added it onto the agenda."

Now she had both boys' full attention. She dropped her voice so that other students at nearby tables couldn't hear.

"I don't want to spread rumors and I sure don't want to start people talking about our Sam," she said. "But you need to know that she's in real trouble. It hasn't gone away just because she showed up at school today."

Andy and Carlos looked worried as they urged her with their eyes to tell them more.

"I think Dr. W has talked her into coming to school each day, but unless we can raise some money, she won't keep coming. She can't afford to. But *we* can't afford to let her down, to not have her here. Right?"

Carlos shifted his gaze between Jett and Andy, his furrowed brow giving him a bewildered expression. "But 'Manita, our school is a public charter magnet school. It's *free!* We don't have to pay a dime to be here."

Andy looked like he had something to say, but he remained silent, staring at her. That was strange. He wasn't dramatic and over the top like Carlos. His reaction made Jett wonder whether he was holding something back.

"What, Andy? Do you know something?"

Andy sighed deeply as he turned to Carlos. "Well, yeah, actually. Look, we don't even think about it because we don't have to, but what Jett's talking about makes sense to me. It *does* cost to be here." Carlos looked like he was struggling to understand as Andy continued. "For example, we don't have a subsidized meal program. And what about how we get here? We don't have dedicated buses because we come from all over. But what if you couldn't afford to get here or to eat?"

All three looked around the Campus Café, which looked more like a bustling urban bistro than a school cafeteria.

Now Carlos just looked affronted. "Aw, come on, man! You mean to tell me that *that* could be the issue? You think *we* need free lunches and rides? We aren't part of some poor inner-city school, you know. We go to Presidio Prep!" At his declaration, Carlos proudly puffed out his chest and waited for them to agree.

Andy face-palmed for a moment as if he couldn't believe what he'd just heard. Jett just felt a deep sense of disappointment that Carlos could be so clueless. Jett knew Andy was a whiz at numbers and always won at Monopoly, so he probably had a better grasp on this money thing than either she or Carlos. But she had hoped for better understanding, for more compassion, from Carlos.

Andy made a guttural sound at the back of his throat. "Carlos, how much did you just spend on your snacks?"

Carlos moaned with irritation. "Okay, already!" He looked pleadingly at Jett. "I don't want to think about it like that. What we gotta do, 'Manita?"

Relieved that Carlos seemed at least open to helping, Jett laid out the plan. "I'm hoping we can convince the PTA to fund a grant for students already at our school who need financial help to stay," she said. "On tonight's agenda, they're voting to select a school for which they will provide financial support. They're already putting together fundraisers for an international school so students can be educated, but what about our own?"

The boys looked at each other and shrugged in unison as they turned back to Jett, and she knew she had their support. For the next several hours, they planned. They plotted. They schemed. They put together a solid argument for taking care of their own community before donating to someone else's. Once they decided what needed to be done and by whom, it was time to go.

Andy looked down at his notes. "I don't think we missed anything."

Daddio's text interrupted their wrap up.

> Kiddo, tell me you guys are on your way. Meeting starts soon.

> Yes.

Notes in hand, the trio packed up and sped across campus to the meeting room. Jett saw three seats saved up front, right next to Daddio. She gave him a grateful smile. Oh, how she loved him. She hoped he knew it.

They were just in time. A striking brunette in a classic navy power suit stepped to the podium and adjusted the mic upwards. She cleared her throat. "As you are no doubt aware, the focus of this meeting is to finalize which deserving school we will sponsor as our sister school. We believe that, with our support, they will be enabled to provide a more inclusive cultural view in their pilot program. This aligns with our leadership mission statement. We have a motion and a second to approve the proposal. All those in favor say—"

Both Dr. W and Daddio held up their hands, interrupting the proceedings. Dismayed, the PTA president glared at them, but neither backed down.

Daddio stood up. "Excuse me, Madame President and," he turned and bowed to the audience behind him, "concerned members of the Presidio Prep community. Before we vote on this very important issue, we ought to consider any conflicting agenda items that may also seek funding. If there are no objections, we have a request ready for presentation." He didn't wait to hear if there were any objections, instead gesturing to Jett and the boys, who rose slowly from their seats. "This is part of the Core5 team that won the freshman project competition last year. They have prepared a request for your consideration tonight. Take it away!"

Jett felt the eyes of the crowd move to them as Andy stepped toward the flustered PTA president. She nodded, at a loss as to what else she could do, and looked stunned as she returned to her seat. They positioned themselves around the microphone.

Carlos started things off. "First of all, I want to make something clear. This is *not* our sophomore presentation. This is *in addition* to what you'll see from us at the end-of-year competition. We plan to win that one, too!"

He stepped aside as Andy came forward, glancing at his notes. "What we'd like to present tonight is how our community can step up and take care of our own before addressing outside needs. It's recently come to our attention that there are some students here at Presidio Prep who are struggling to survive—not academically, but *literally* to survive..."

In a strong, measured cadence, Andy laid out their case before the community. Jett watched as understanding slowly dawned on their faces. Andy refuted each viable concern, artfully leading them to the same conclusion she had helped the boys reach earlier that afternoon. Jett couldn't help but beam with pride, just like her Daddio. Andy ended his presentation with a request for questions, but the room was practically silent. Then an indistinct murmur rumbled through the meeting. It seemed to Jett that many had never considered that *their* student body included students struggling to make ends meet.

While the audience worked to digest this new proposal, Dr. W used the opportunity to show his support for their request. He redirected the focus to a detailed plan that not only funded this new proposal but also left room for some of the original sister school funding.

Dr. W's plan was adopted and ratified within an hour. Within two hours, they funded it to the tune of $450,000, just from those in attendance.

Jett knew there would be more funding soon. Wait until the Presidio Prep people who weren't at the meeting learned about this new initiative! They would help, too—wouldn't they? They could already do so much with what they had in hand. It was almost overwhelming, but in a good way. Jett couldn't stop smiling as a medley of emotions danced inside her body.

And the best news—her favorite part—was that this was more proof her school really cared about their own community. It wasn't just a publicity stunt. To her, this was about the community getting their priorities straight. The student body mattered. The parents and teachers at this meeting just showed that. People vote with their money. They would take care of their own—and Sam would be safe.

23

THE TRIO WALKED out with both Daddio and Dr. W, knowing exactly who would be funded first.

"Hey, Daddio! Dr. W! Can we go save Sam now?" Jett was grinning from ear to ear. The boys stood by her side. Their parents emerged from the crowd, watching with avid interest. Carlos and Andy each took a step back to stand with their parents.

Carlos' dad cuffed him gently on the arm. "I see! So, this was close to home, as mi esposa suspected." He smiled at Jett and then put out his hand towards her. "Well done!" Abruptly, his face fell. "Unfortunately, my Carlito has to get a good night's sleep tonight and cannot be out too late. Game tomorrow." He ushered his son away, but looked over his shoulder as they departed, adding, "but I want to see more of you all. Soon. We shall host a party to welcome in the summer!" With an enthusiastic wave, the family was off.

Jett wondered if he meant it and hoped that he had seen her nod in agreement. These adults all seemed to keep their word. Look at how they had stepped up for this new grant.

Off to one side, Andy's parents were speaking quietly together. Jett watched his father squeeze his mother's hand with affection. Then he spoke in a quiet, self-possessed manner to their group. "Thank you for allowing us to witness the ways your school culture has affected our Anand. We are proud of what we saw tonight, and only sorry that the evening must end for us as well. We need to get home." His smile was radiant and infectious.

Andy's mother embraced Jett as she whispered in her ear. "Please come see us again soon, Jett. Dadi and Nani both are asking for you." She patted Jett's shoulder and smiled as she pulled away. Jett felt warm, as if the hug still lingered.

She just couldn't stop smiling! Jett turned to the two adults who remained. "Well, Dr. W and Daddio! Can we go take care of this right now, please? We need to tell Sam—and Grams! She'll be so happy that Sam started a whole movement and had such an impact on our school!"

Dr. W started nodding, then stopped. "Maybe," he said slowly. "I think it might depend on how it's presented."

Jett saw that he seemed to be thinking things through.

After a few moments, he decided. "Okay, Jett. I agree we shouldn't wait to share the good news. But it's getting late, so we need to keep it short. Will you allow me and your father to handle this? I'd like to call it the Presidio Prep Outstanding Student Grant and maybe talk about Sam's extraordinary singing to emphasize how much we need her in our community. Okay? Will you allow me to take the lead?"

Without hesitation, Jett agreed. What was most important was that Sam and Grams accepted. She knew how private Sam could be. Jett didn't want to do anything that would stop her best friend from receiving the help she needed. A merit-based grant was a solid way to accomplish that goal.

"Yes, Doc! Please. That's brilliant, actually." She glanced at her father. "Daddio, are you driving? We should get going now. You know where they are, right?" With a quick salute of acknowledgement, Daddio lead Dr. W toward the car.

SOON THEY WERE standing in a dimly lit hallway in front of an apartment door. Daddio double-checked the address on his phone and nodded before she knocked.

Sam opened the door and stepped back. Jett couldn't tell which kind of shock showed on Sam's face, the happy kind or the worried kind. That made little sense to Jett, though, so she decided to act as if it could only be the happy kind.

"Hi, Sam," Dr. W said as he stepped forward. "Is your grandmother here?"

Sam turned her body as if to block the view into the apartment and dropped her voice to a low whisper. "I told you I would find a way to come to class each day." She looked at the trio with a mixture of alarm and annoyance. "I need you to trust me on that. Now isn't a good time."

Just then, another voice floated into the hallway. "Samantha? Child, who is at the door?" Her voice broke. "We have three days! They can't be back already. I need to pack."

Shoulders slumped, Sam hung her head and moved back in defeat. She opened the door wider. Jett thought she heard crying. As they entered, she realized she was right. Grams was crying. Jett didn't know what to do. Did Daddio and Dr. W know how to respond?

Dr. W stepped smoothly into the apartment and crouched down in front of Grams, who was huddled in a small armchair. She looked at him through a watery smile as he gently took her hand.

"Hello there, son. I'm afraid I don't know you."

"Yes, ma'am, you don't yet. I am Dr. Jefferson Smith Williams. My people are from Richmond and I'm lucky enough to work with the student body at Presidio Prep." Keeping his light touch on her hand, he tilted his head toward the other visitors. "This is Mr. Harper and his daughter, Jett. I believe you have already met them."

Grams nodded, even as Jett thought she saw a look of confusion cross her face. Sam crossed the room quickly and took her other hand.

"Well, doctor, thank you for coming to see us, but I'm a bit confused." She glanced shakily out the dark window. "It's pretty late for an impromptu house call. Is there something I can help you with? Did my Samantha do something wrong? She's a very responsible girl. I can't fathom what…" Her brow was crinkled.

Jett was finding it increasingly hard to stay silent.

Fortunately, Doc responded quickly to her confusion.

Jett noticed he squeezed Grams' hand before he did so. Was that something you could do to signal you were going to interrupt? Jett would need to think about that later. She liked holding hands.

"Ms.—I'm sorry I don't know your name. May I please call you Grams?"

Still looking anxious, Grams nodded.

"Grams, I am sorry to interrupt, but we have such good news that we couldn't wait to come over and tell you." He smiled broadly at her, turning slightly to include Sam in his joy. "Your granddaughter is an important member of our school community. She probably didn't know it, but she's been in the running for a special award for a while now. Today in my office, Sam sang and confirmed her eligibility. Tonight at the PTA meeting, under the recommendation of myself and Mr. Harper, Sam won the award."

Grams put her hand to her heart and sat back. "Oh, my goodness! Oh, *my*!" She turned to Sam, detaching her hand from Dr. W's to quickly wipe at the tears lingering on her cheeks. "See what staying in school and working on your education does? Just *look* at what happened. You won an award! And at your fancy city school! Your Mama and Daddy never did that. *You* did that! Baby girl, I am so proud of you! I am so—" Trembling, she reached for her granddaughter, who bent down to accept her fierce hug as Dr. Williams stood back.

Sam tried to whisper only to Grams, but Jett heard clearly in the tight quarters. "Yeah, but I can't stay *now*, can I? We have bigger things to think about. You need me. We have three days …"

Grams swatted at her. "Child, hush now. Three days is more than enough time for another miracle! Your award was the first. Can't you just take a moment and thank the Lord for your blessings?"

Sam looked frustrated as she stroked Grams' shoulder.

Jett couldn't stand it anymore. "Sam, are you quitting on us?"

Giving Jett a quick look of warning, Dr. W interjected. "There's more you need to know," he said quickly. "Even though there is no ceremony, in order to accept this merit grant, you have to make a commitment. Are you willing to hear us out? You could reject it."

Jett walked right up to Dr. W and placed a hand over his mouth. "No. You can*not* reject it. You are not allowed." She glared at Dr. W before turning back to her best friend. "Just agree, okay? We need you. *I* need you. Just say yes!"

Sam looked like she was trying hard not to laugh out loud at Jett's action. The look in her eyes made Jett realize she'd gone and done it again—something others wouldn't have. But it needed to be done, so what was the big deal? She took her hand off of Dr. W's lips, who stood mutely looking stunned. Jett muttered an apology as she shrugged and stepped back. She wasn't *really* sorry, but that seemed like the right thing to do. Although she retreated into waiting mode, this time she was ready to spring into action if they didn't get this right.

It was Daddio's turn to intercede. "Hi, Grams. Sorry for all the late-night drama," he said, crouching down in front of her. "You know how teenagers can be, though. Jett was just too excited to let this news sit all night and, frankly, so are we. What the good doc here didn't get a chance to say was that this award comes with a full scholarship, including housing and travel expenses backdated to acceptance into the Presidio Prep community."

Grams cried out and started fanning herself as she slumped back in the chair. Everyone jumped into action.

"Grams!" Sam gripped her shoulders and turned to Jett. "Go to the kitchen and get her some water."

Jett ran into the tiny but spotless kitchen and opened cupboards until she spotted three small glasses. She quickly filled one at the sink and wondered if she should bring anything else. There didn't seem to be anything else to bring, so—glass of water in hand—she returned to the living room. She heard Grams speaking softly. It sounded like a prayer.

Sam glanced at Jett and put a finger to her lips. Jett stayed quiet as Daddio took the water from her. He waited for the right moment to offer it to Grams, who was crying and laughing and saying all kinds of things that didn't make contextual sense to Jett. Things like "Praise Jesus," "God is great," and "thank you, Lord."

Jett felt the palpable release of the tension that had blanketed the whole place just a little while ago. She shrugged. It must be all right. Jett realized she would have to ask someone about Grams' proclamations later to understand them.

Sam took her aside as Daddio and the doc continued to minister to Grams. She spoke urgently, her voice filled with hope, even as she tried to hide it. "Is this for real? I mean, not a handout, but a *real* award?"

Jett nodded emphatically. "It is!" she enthused. "They voted tonight. It's yours! I don't have the official application memorized, but I'm pretty sure it's because you're so, so smart! You know how to work in a team. And you give voice to things I can't even begin to name. You can make grownups cry and laugh. You even started teaching me to use my voice. Will you do that some more? The way you sing is magic. You *have* to stay." She looked pleadingly into Sam's eyes. "You'll stay now, right? Please? Tell me this means—"

Sam threw herself at Jett. "Shut up already, Dorothy! Of course I'll stay! I'll need help, but we can do this. Right?"

Jett offered muffled agreement as Sam continued to embrace her, fighting to sift through the tears that clogged her throat. Until that moment, she hadn't realized how worried she'd been that Sam would refuse the money. Now that she'd accepted it, Jett felt like she could breathe again.

Pulling apart at last only to link arms, Sam and Jett turned around to the tail-end of a conversation between the three grownups. Grams handed Daddio a three-day eviction notice. He solemnly took it and promised he would handle it. Sam was safe for now. It was time to go.

As Sam softly closed the door behind them, Jett felt exultant. She looked at her Daddio, who was also smiling, and then at Dr. W, whose smile had faded away. He seemed lost in thought.

On the street, the doc paused and turned his focus on Daddio. "I can take an Uber from here," he said, "but before I go, I've got a question, Mr. Harper." He studied Daddio for a long moment. "Did you really just promise Grams that the grant would cover a year of back rent and Sam's travel expenses?"

Daddio nodded. Jett felt a tremor of anxiety.

"You know we aren't authorized to offer that, right? We can only offer from tonight forward because there wasn't even a fund until tonight."

Daddio kept nodding. Jett took hold of his arm to steady herself. She felt so confused. Did Daddio just break the cardinal rule of under-promise and over-deliver?

Daddio put his arm around her and pulled her in close as she gazed up at him. Although silent, her eyes held questions that he didn't yet see. Instead, he spoke to Dr. W.

"It's true the official grant can't offer that, but *I* can," he replied. "My firm will absorb it and give that woman some breathing room. Grams and Sam both deserve it." Finally, he met his daughter's gaze. "What she has given us—given to Jett—is worth more than that to me. I mean to ensure Sam sticks around."

Doc W's expression shifted slowly to admiration as this news sunk in.

"All right, then. I won't spoil it by telling," he said, his grin broadening by the minute. "You know, Mr. Harper, you have a real reputation for your approach to the law, the rules, and how things work. I'll admit it intimidated me when I first learned who you were. But I respect a man who quietly sets about changing the world. I can see where Jett gets her heart. Thank you."

A few minutes later, the smile that lit Doc's face as he entered his rideshare could have lit up city blocks. As Doc rode away, Joe Harper gave his daughter a tender look before turning his attention to the apartment buildings on either side of them. He squeezed Jett more tightly to his side.

"It's time to go home, Jettster. You ready?"

"Yes, thank you, Daddio," she replied with a long sign of contentment. "I am."

24

WITH ANOTHER SCHOOL year almost over, a wide range of student patrons spilled in and out of the Campus Café. Many study groups and knots of friends crammed around too-small tables. These two groups were almost indistinguishable, unless you knew what to look for—and Jett was pretty sure Ruby, reigning Queen of Teen Culture, knew *exactly* what to look for. Her minions could tell you, too.

Ruby was a superstar on the rise, even with her mysterious absence from daily physical interactions. All of her media feeds focused on teaching the world something she deemed essential. Her latest mission? Teaching the masses about Good, Better, and Best. Everyone could see that Ruby had it all. She was the Best.

A buzz of surprise and excitement electrified the air everywhere but at the Core5 table as Ruby swept into the cafe. She was back and, thanks to Carlos, their little cohort had expected it. He had kept them updated about

Ruby's stalkers being identified and subdued. A few suspects were under investigation and an arrest was expected soon. Now Ruby wanted her life back. Entourage in tow, she approached the table where Carlos was acting up, Sam and Andy were laughing, and Jett was quietly looking on, waiting to get back on track.

Ruby's singsong greeting practically whistled. "Hello! Anyone here? I mean, anyone observant, important, ready to win the end-of-year challenge... *here*?" She looked each team member in the eye, calling them out, as her Vipers laughed.

Carlos jumped up. "Linda, mi vida! You're back!" He gestured broadly to the group. "We are all so glad!"

"Oh, come off it, Carlos," Sam said teasingly. "She doesn't care about you any more than she does the rest of us, and I'm not 'so glad' she's back. It was nice when she wasn't stirring up trouble."

Ruby huffed, and her crowd fell back. Only her personal bodyguard—a strapping blonde Romeo in a close-fitted sport jacket that dressed up his immaculate white t-shirt—stepped forward. Ruby stopped him with her hand raised and a look until he blended back into the crowd.

"*Really?*" she shot back at Sam. "This is the thanks I get for putting myself in danger to find *you*?" Ruby tossed her glistening locks around and pouted.

Jett felt obligated to do something fast to diffuse the mounting tension. But Ruby was on a roll.

"Hey, Andy, what happened to your old glasses? At least those made you look kind of hipster cool," she sneered. "This pair makes you look like a freak and a geek. Should I just pick one? Or are you both?"

Oh, *hell* no. After everything they'd been through, Jett wasn't about to let her team dissolve. As she struggled to imagine the best, most biting way to respond, Sam beat her to the punch. Springing out of her seat, Sam got into Ruby's face.

"Excuse me?"

Jett flashed on that first day of freshman year when Sam reminded her of a sleek black cat. Claws out now, she was ready to fight but Ruby didn't move back. Instead, she grinned.

"Yes! You poor little wannabe, I'll excuse you," she purred smoothly. "*This time.* In the meantime, do you need a refresher on how things work around here?" Ruby waved her manicured hand at the group as if she owned the world.

That was *IT*. Jett couldn't hold back a moment longer. "Ruby."

Slowly, pointedly, Ruby turned her attention regally on Jett.

Narrow-eyed, Jett advanced slowly between Ruby and Sam, keeping her eyes locked on Ruby's. "I'm glad you're safe enough to join your team finally, but why are all those people here?" Jett pointed at Ruby's sycophants with her chin. "Do you need them to protect you," she batted her eyelashes rapidly and put a hand on her chest, "from us?"

"Oh, them?" Ruby glanced at her minions dismissively. "Are *you* kidding now, Jett? Did you learn how to make a joke while I was away?" She abruptly turned away, inspecting her nails with studied casualness. "You've already met some of them," she added, raising an eyebrow at Jett as if daring her to remember.

How could Jett forget? Narrowing her eyes, Jett assumed Ruby was referring to the Vipers, the mean girls who did their best to never miss a minute of Ruby's life, the ones known for their brazen bullying of everyone they could.

Ruby nodded when she knew Jett got it. "As for the newbs? They're my handlers, my new team. It's the price you pay for true stardom. Others must circle your orbit." Ruby sighed. "You'll get used to them. After all, they go with me everywhere now. It's their life."

Jett was startled. Was Ruby talking about slaves? "But—"

Ruby shook her head. "No 'buts.' It's the truth and the way it is." She turned back to the rest of the team. "Now—what happened while I was gone? Did you finish our presentation? I only gave one assignment." She looked pointedly at Jett. "And you failed."

Jett's jaw dropped open. One assignment? As in, when Ruby asked her to text? She couldn't possibly mean that. But she did.

"Since Jett never even texted me *once*, I'm assuming you guys floundered through and put together something less-than-stellar on my topic," she said, waving a hand at them dismissively. "I mean, it's not like you guys could become experts like me in the short time I was away."

Hands on hips, she glared at them, waiting. When no one handed her any material, she propped a hand on the table and began drumming her fingernails loudly. "Now let me seI'm sure there might be *something* I could incorporate," she said with a note of exasperation.

At this, Sam started laughing. Andy smiled at the sound. Carlos was shaking his head in disbelief, and Jett realized her mouth was still hanging open. She closed it, swallowed, and tried again.

"Ruby, we dropped that. Months ago. Jett looked at the Core, who all stood behind her, literally backing her up. "You were gone. We decided to focus on safety. Ms. Diaz approved the change. I thought—"

Ruby exploded. "Hold up. You changed *my* presentation without consulting *me*? And Ms. Diaz *approved*?" Livid red crept from her throat to her face. "I know she told my tutors it was all in hand, but no one mentioned you cut me out. What do you guys even know about danger or safety?"

Ruby turned to her devotees. "Can you believe this?" Gesticulating wildly to the heavens above, she revved up her performance. "I'm gone so I can single-handedly save Sam *and* subdue the stalker situation—while still maintaining top grades, I might add—and *this* is the thanks I get? I honestly don't know what to say!"

"Um, you say 'thank you,'" Sam interjected. "And while you're at it, you say that you learned along the way that the whole world doesn't revolve around you."

One sycophant laughed softly, breaking off the moment Ruby spun around to see who would dare to do such a thing. She drew herself up to her full height, breathing heavily. Silence descended on the entire cafe.

Jett, desperate to get the situation back on track, tried to placate her. "Look, Ruby. We're glad you're back." She stopped and surveyed the growing audience. "Can you tell them to go? We have work to do and things to decide."

Ruby squinted, looked around, and then shooed off the crowd with a wave of her hand before pinning Jett with a glare. In a small but clear voice, Ruby demanded, "I *told you* to text. Why didn't you text?"

Jett saw Sam take a breath as if to respond and sent her a nearly imperceptible shake of her head to let Sam know she shouldn't interfere.

Taking a deep breath in, Jett faced Ruby squarely. "I didn't text you, Ruby, it's true," she said, feeling sincerely sorry. "I said I would and I just never quite… it was always… well, I didn't. I'm sorry for that." For just a moment, she saw the hurt in Ruby's eyes. The naked longing and loneliness were astounding. Jett gasped.

Ruby turned away.

Jett stepped closer. "I really didn't mean—"

Spine straight, hand up to stop the words, Ruby didn't turn. "Don't. Just don't. I don't know why I expected more of you."

Jett's shoulders slumped and she stumbled back. Andy and Carlos both stepped up to balance her. Jett caught the verbal blow in her gut but kept silent. She knew she deserved Ruby's disappointment. But this? This hit harder than she expected.

"Hold on there, Princess High-and-Mighty." Sam rounded the space quickly until she was standing directly in front of Ruby. "I know you think you're all that, but seriously, did you even *once* stop to consider that maybe something else was going on besides the world that revolves around you?" Sam stared her down with a look of sheer disgust. "You have *no idea* what happened to us while you were away at some luxury spa!"

Arms crossed across her chest, Ruby smirked.

Jett started to say something but Sam breathed in deeply and mimicked Ruby's signature posture, chest lifted and hands on her own hips. "I won't have you waltzing in a day before our presentation, demanding to know if we've done *our* part to make *you* look good!" Sam looked at the other members of the Core5. "Is she even a part of us anymore? Are we honestly going to let her walk in here and use our work for her own gain?"

Carlos's eyebrows shot up and his lips turned down. He shrugged and stepped back, deferring to Andy, who was studying the ground before he spoke. "I don't think so," he said solemnly. "I think we need to take a vote. Are we a Core5 or Core4 now?"

"Core5, always and forever." Carlos had recovered from his momentary confusion. "One team. Don't forget *you* were gone too, Sam."

"But I'm here now and since I got back, I've been working nonstop to make up the difference," she shot back. "I say Core4. Cut off the deadwood. One team, only stronger."

The four moved closer to debate without Ruby's interference. Every time Jett looked at Ruby, she saw the unease radiating from her. Jett remembered the loneliness and fear hidden behind Ruby's facade.

"We're deadlocked," Sam said, addressing Ruby again. "If I'm going to change my vote so you can come back, I want to know one thing. And I mean the whole thing—*honestly*—from start to finish and then we will vote again."

Arms crossed over her chest, Ruby nodded curtly. "Okay. *One* thing. What is it?"

"I want to hear about your stalker and how you found safety," Sam said with a grin. "What do you know about real life—about fear and tough choices? I want to know *your* story."

Ruby swallowed. She eyed her old teammates one by one before turning to speak quietly with her bodyguard. As she returned to the Core, he dispersed the waiting fans. Suddenly the Core5 had privacy and Ruby spilled. When she was done, no one broke the spell by speaking.

Andy had accepted Ruby's apology as Jett stood by his side. Carlos squeezed Ruby's hand and she gave him a small smile. Jett thought she saw her squeeze back. Sam's face curled as she chewed on her bottom lip. Silently, she did a recount by looking into each team member's eyes. *Now* it was unanimous. They were a Core5.

Ruby was part of the team once again.

25

ON THE NIGHT of the Sophomore Sound-Off, parents, faculty, students, and contestants packed the auditorium. All watched with rapt attention. Judges congregated to evaluate not only which team presented well, as they had for their freshman challenge, but also the issue that caught the attention of each team.

Jett couldn't focus. She didn't watch the competition. She was caught up in *one* detail. Jett kept thinking about the name. All this time, she had thought that Pick Your Focus was the name of the challenge, not Sophomore Sound-Off. Did that mean the presentation was more important than the subject? She thought both were to be weighed equally. Had her team gotten it all wrong? She tried to refocus, but it was hard.

Each member of her Core5 was expressing nervousness in different ways. In the back, Sam was pacing. Andy was quietly observing. Carlos was joking with his soccer teammates, staying connected but not to the Core. And Ruby? Ruby was laser-focused, watching each presentation through narrowed, judgemental eyes.

For the first time, Jett understood the adage 'if looks could kill' because she was sure that if any look could do so, it would be the one on Ruby's face. She would be a murderer. Murderer or murderess? Which term applied? Gah! Her mind latched onto this other detail and she couldn't let it go. Until, that is, Ruby tried none too gently to get her attention, which only increased Jett's angst.

"Psst! Earth to Jett! Seriously! Earth to Jett!"

Then, for a blessed moment, Ruby was quiet and Jett's internal pressure let up slightly. When she realized the rest of the team surrounded her, it ratcheted up again. Uh-oh. Had she blacked out? No. She had been lost in thought about scary Ruby, the murderer/murderess with the homicidal stare. Staring at the ground, Jett offered a small smile to her team to match the shrug of her shoulders.

A sigh of relief escape from someone but before Jett could figure out the source, Ruby took up her entire field of vision. Oh no. Here it was.

"What's your problem, Jett? I need you to focus." Ruby snapped her fingers in front of Jett's face. "Focus on me!"

Jett chuckled softly. That was the problem; it's *exactly* what she had been doing.

Ruby whirled around to the team. "See? I think she's lost it. *Again!* What are we going to do? This is serious."

"Bonita, she is fine," Carlos soothed. "Jett is just thinking. She is a deep thinker, you know. Give her a moment."

Jett saw Carlos' brotherly concern in the way he looked at her. She reached out for his hand and smiled at him. She had no words for how grateful she was for his faith in her. Carlos, her pretend brother and first everywhere friend.

Looking irritated when he saw that Jett and Carlos were holding hands, Andy interceded. "She's fine, Ruby. Give her a little space. Like this." He moved Ruby aside. When she didn't move back to her original spot, he crouched slightly, put his hands on his knees and looked Jett in the eye. "Do you need water? Or to breathe? Or… or *anything?*"

Jett shook her head no and let go of Carlos' hand to give Andy a hug. He beamed and she could feel the warmth rising in Andy's tight embrace. Right now, there was no place she'd rather be than here, giving him a hug. She heard Sam take a stab at Ruby.

"Okay, Drama Mama. What's this really all about? What has *you* in such a snit?"

Ruby's arms were crossed over her chest. Jett watched her eyes dart around at her team members before she let out a breath and stood up straighter. "I just realized something. You guys aren't going to like it, but it has to be said." She set her jaw and lifted her chin. "Have you been listening to what our competition has been saying? Notice anything?"

The other members of the Core5 glanced at each other in confusion.

Ruby threw her hands up in the air. "Seriously? No one but *me* caught this?" She let out a sound of disgust. "Okay, well, what we have in common with everyone else is that we have a bunch of well-researched facts and statistics. Everyone does. Where we *really* differ, though, is that we're the *only* ones addressing a huge, uncomfortable subject that won't be tied up neatly at the end of our presentation. We've got plenty of facts but no solutions." Ruby stopped to let this sink in.

Carlos looked at Sam, who looked at Andy, who looked at Jett before they all turned back to Ruby.

"We have a problem and *we* know it's personal, but no one else here does. And *we haven't solved it*."

Jett frowned as she nodded slowly, taking it all in. This was a very valid point. With everything going on this school year, her team had tackled something big—*truly monumental*—that had escaped not only the notice but also the experience of their classmates. Jett knew that this was no time to pretend that there were easy solutions.

So, *this* was the time to 'get real' then—even in front of a packed auditorium. *Yikes!* An idea started forming in her head and she held up a hand to be given a moment to work it through. When Jett had ordered her thinking, she took in a loud, deep breath and looked Ruby in the eye. "Thank you, Ruby. You're right."

Caught completely off guard, Ruby grinned before looking around. She shrugged her shoulders and reapplied her mask of nonchalance.

"Of course I am! But what are we going to do?"

All eyes were on Jett, who smiled calmly because she knew the answer.

"*We've* already got it," she said confidently. "Here's what we're going to do."

They huddled in close to hear the updated plan. Finally, they stood up, nodding and smiling. No time to rehearse. They were up next.

"Ruby, you're first," Jett said.

"Ha! I knew *that!*" she responded with her typical smirk.

Strutting like a fashion model on a catwalk, she led the way onto the stage.

Ruby stuck out her hip, planted a hand on it, and took control. "Thank you for being here and for giving us your time and attention. We've heard some pretty convincing presentations to 'fake it until you make it' and about 'happiness being a choice.' But what if it isn't always—a choice, I mean. Today our team, *my* Core5, of which I am immensely proud to be a part, is seeking safety. And while we don't want to bring you all down, we *do* want to get real. Because this matters to every single one of us."

Ruby moved over slightly to give Sam room at the podium.

"We've lived three years inside of these last nine months," Sam said. "One member of our team faced severe isolation and loneliness while stalkers followed her every move and threatened her safety. One member faced the tough choice of keeping a roof over her family's heads or going to school so she could break the cycle of poverty holding them back. Two of our members were physically assaulted because of the color of their skin, even though they were doing *everything* right."

Sam hesitated, glancing back at Jett before continuing. "And last, but not least, we have a member of our team who we all watch out for her because her body, her system, randomly shuts down without warning. "I can't tell you what *that's* about, because I don't know. But what I *do* know is that our Core5 lives in danger every single day and we are seeking safety."

With Jett between them, Carlos and Andy each holding a hand, the remaining trio stepped up to join Ruby and Sam. The boys presented the group's data. They also shared their concerns, and filled in some of what happened to their team this last year, without sharing any names.

Then it was Jett's turn. She looked down into the sea of intent faces and swallowed hard. This was not to script and that took courage. Proud of them, but knowing it was her turn, Jett tried to not panic. Time to enter the arena. Jett nodded solemnly at each of her teammates as she took the mic.

"As a normal fifteen-year-old, I didn't expect to confront the issues of celebrity stalkers, racial profiling, or devastating poverty. I knew about the health issues because it's how I'm wired. I've been dealing with it my whole life. But until now, I never saw it as a safety issue, too. I figured I was good. I just had to be a little more careful than my peers." She stopped, closed her eyes for a moment, breathed. Then she opened her eyes and leaned closer to the microphone. "I've learned how wrong that assumption is and I've learned that we're better, stronger, *safer* together. It isn't the solution to these very real, very grown-up issues, but it is a step. Please join us in making this step. We urge you to build your own team. Create *your* Core5 and look out for one another. *Our* Core5 wants to build a whole community of Core5s, linked together by the shared belief of 'people over problems.' Want to join us?"

Hands shot up. A roar of applause met her request and she watched as everyone rose to their feet. Startled, she didn't know what to do. She took a step back and blew out the breath she hadn't realized she was holding. Andy squeezed her hand and she realized her entire Core5 was holding hands—even Ruby and Sam. She hadn't seen that coming. She looked out again at the roaring audience. This was overwhelming. After sharing all these truths, Jett could feel her body shutting down. She felt completely used up, overworked, spent. She needed to find a place to melt. Jett wanted home.

26

IN THE CAR, on the way home after winning the Sophomore Sound-Off, Mother spoke first. "Huh. Interesting." Her jaw tightened and she pursed her lips. "I didn't expect that. You went for the sympathy vote: 'poor little broken girl.' Well, I guess it worked."

And just like that, Mother shrugged off an entire school year of work. Stunned, Jett retreated within herself. She studied Daddio's hands. As he gripped the steering wheel, his knuckles turned white. As he turned quickly toward his wife, it looked to Jett like he, too, was in shock. Like a song on repeat, the words "poor little broken girl," "poor little broken girl" kept playing in Jett's head. She couldn't believe what Mother had just said and she couldn't unhear it.

But Kathy wasn't done twisting her knife. "You want to learn about safety? You want to hear about danger? About *real* danger?" She looked at her husband. "Tell her what happened right before we left for her little school thing."

Joe was silent, his hands twisted around the steering wheel as if he could break it. Kathy, her hands folded gracefully in her lap, seemed cool and in command. Her dispassionate voice went on, shooting shards of hurt into Jett.

"A detective came to the house asking questions about our strange neighbor—that Ben person."

Joe uttered a low, guttural growl. "Not now, Kathy. I'm warning you—"

She pressed on as if he hadn't said a word. "The detective said that neighbor Ben had been in conversion therapy for years and they had to escalate his treatment plan several times."

With a sad little tsk-tsking sound, Mother shook her head. "Apparently, he *ran away* from the family who loved him so much. He cut all ties and moved to *our* neighborhood. Can you believe it? Can you *imagine*? Ben isn't even his *real* name." She turned slightly toward Jett, reveling in the drama and carnage as she carved pain into the moment. "Someone found him tonight," she said. "That's why he's at Marin General now. Someone *literally* tried to beat some sense into him."

Beyond the roaring in her ears, Jett tried to figure out what Mother was talking about. This couldn't be right. She seemed so removed. How could she say something like that and remain so unaffected? *Even if* Mother didn't like Ben, he was *still* a human being *and* her daughter's friend!

Jett's breathing was labored, even as her body flooded with adrenaline, putting her on high alert. She needed to know more. But she wanted to know less. None of that mattered. She needed to get to Ben. In a broken whisper, Jett asked everything with one word. "Daddio?"

She didn't recognize her own voice, but apparently he did.

"On it, kiddo." Tight-lipped and turning red, Joe pulled over to the side of the road. He reached over and undid Mother's seatbelt before stretching across her and opening the car door. "Kathy, out. You can walk from here. Or call a damn car. Your choice. Jett and I are late. We've got somewhere to be."

Sputtering in protest and with one long, angry look at her husband, she got out of his car and stood in shock on the sidewalk. Daddio didn't hesitate. He slammed the door shut and sped away.

"Lovebug, we're on it. We're going to see Ben."

MARIN GENERAL WAS a ten-minute drive and they were halfway there when Daddio broke the silence.

"Kiddo, I know this makes no sense," he said in a low, soothing voice. "You just pulled off a major win and we should be celebrating with ice cream somewhere. But your mom—," his voice broke slightly as he stopped and dragged in a deep breath. "I believe she really *does* want to help you understand life the way she does. You know, she gets paid a lot of money to help people understand. I think she's hurting that you guys are so far apart."

Jett made a noise of protest, but Daddio held up a hand.

"Just let me say this. I know it sounds like I'm making excuses for her. I'm not. *Really*. And I'm sorry she can be so... so *unaware* of how her messages come across," he rushed on. "She can be so stubborn about what she's researched and all the theories she believes. Your mom goes down a path and then it's hard for her to turn back around–"

Daddio trailed off as he gave Jett a small smile in the rearview mirror. "Know anyone else like that?" After pointing a quick finger at both of them, he shrugged and laughed to himself. "Yeah, not you, not me—Anyway, I hope you know that she really, really loves you. I mean it. Your mom goes out of her mind trying to figure out how to show you love. And I know she fails, but it's there. I promise."

And with that, he fell silent again, focusing through the windshield on the street racing past around them.

Jett knew she should accept his words at face value, but she couldn't. She knew she should forgive Mother. But she reasoned that she was just a 15-year-old kid. She wanted to forgive. She wanted to feel Mother's love, to believe Daddio and to have all this pain heal. Jett considered learning how to forgive as a possible summer project. Could she do it? She didn't know. Right now, in this moment, she just knew that she had to get to Ben.

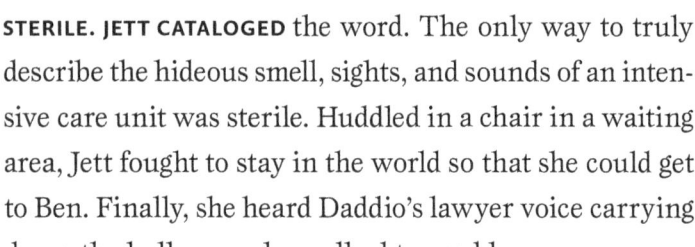

STERILE. JETT CATALOGED the word. The only way to truly describe the hideous smell, sights, and sounds of an intensive care unit was sterile. Huddled in a chair in a waiting area, Jett fought to stay in the world so that she could get to Ben. Finally, she heard Daddio's lawyer voice carrying down the hallway as he walked toward her.

"Thank you, Nurse Katie. My brother will appreciate you letting us in. I'll talk to my daughter and let her know what you've told me." He came into view and crouched down next to her. "Kiddo, your Uncle Ben can't respond and we don't know how much he can hear. This kind nurse says us talking to him will be important. Can you do that? Ignore what you see and just talk to him?" Daddio seemed to be inspecting her, testing her defenses.

Jett nodded mutely. She didn't understand why Daddio was calling Ben his brother or her uncle. It was the first she'd heard of it. Was he really? Daddio didn't have siblings, at least none that she knew of. Was this something Daddio had said to get past the nurse, like they did on a TV show? Jett felt the weight of two sets of eyes assessing her, waiting for her answer. Could she ignore whatever she saw and talk to Ben? Well, *duh*. If that is what it took for her to see her friend *and* it would help him, she could talk all night. She had so much to tell him.

It was Nurse Katie's turn to lean into Jett's field of

view. "Honey, your uncle may look a little different, a little scary, even. I just want you to know that. He's still the same person, even when the outside looks different, okay?"

"What should we be prepared for?" Joe asked quietly.

The nurse shook her head. "I can't tell you much, but you'll see they broke every bone in his beautiful face, so his head is misshapen. You'll also see a lot of bruising." The nurse stopped and seemed to wait for something.

Jett thought the pause might be so this information could sink in, but she simply found it irritating. She wanted to see Ben. Now.

The nurse turned Joe away and dropped to a whisper, but Jett still could hear everything she said. "Do you really think she can handle this? Just as importantly, can *you?*" She patted his arm soothingly. "I mean, if you *can*, it's better for him to have loved ones around, but if you go in and figure out that you *can't*, it'll be worse. He needs peace and quiet and, most of all, acceptance. Can you give him that?"

Daddio reached for Jett's hand and they both nodded. She knew they would, regardless of whether they could. They *would*. Jett's whole body tensed as she steeled herself for the unknown. She hated the unknown.

Satisfied, Nurse Katie steered them down the hall and into a room that held only one bed. Jett pushed through the door, rushing to see her friend, still totally unprepared.

Halfway into the room, Daddio right behind her, Jett stopped. She wasn't sure the person, the body in the bed, was even totally human. She saw someone attached via multiple wires and tubes to a network of machines. His face was so swollen, it looked like bad special effects makeup had been applied. Jett wondered how this could be *anyone's* reality, let alone Ben's.

Unfamiliar equipment signaled something. Should she be worried? What did that mean and where was the nurse? Jett squinted. She was sure others could hear it, that beep-beep-beeping.

Overhead lights emphasized the desolate darkness around Ben's bed. The incessant beeps bounced around the room like a broken metronome. The lights, the sounds, the mood, everything was low, except the pain and fear amplified in Jett's head. How do you prepare for and process something you've never seen and couldn't ever imagine?

Daddio stepped up next to her, taking her hand. He didn't try to move her. He just stood there—her rock—supporting her and keeping his eyes trained on Ben's unconscious body. After a few minutes, Daddio stirred.

"Jett, honey," he whispered. "This is a lot. We can go or stay—whichever you need."

Jett squeezed his hand, hoping he would know she meant "thank you." She was having a hard time reconciling what she saw with what she knew. Leaving might not make it easier, but she couldn't figure out whether to stay and face this or go home and process. Her body shook with the effort to contain her tears.

Jett looked at the bed. Time to assess. What did she know? She knew a man was lying there, but was it really *her* Ben? Timidly, she took one step closer. Stretching up onto the balls of her feet, she inspect the broken body. She looked for signs of her favorite neighbor. Swollen like a sponge left in water, this man's head was shaved in places. She saw stitches. Every inch of visible skin was discolored, showing discordant patterns. He didn't look like Ben and she wished he wasn't, but she knew he was. The patient information posted nearby said so. No amount of wishing would change reality. Jett took another step closer.

She wanted to touch him, but there were so many wires and cords. One hand had tape and ports attached through the top, but the other was free. Discolored and fragile, but with long tapered fingers she knew—those were Ben's hands. She had to face it. Jett stared at the hand that had first guided her toward the puppy-with-no-name and her vision blurred with tears she wouldn't let spill. Slowly, carefully, she reached out and tucked her hand underneath his own.

"Hello, Chum. I feel so glum," she murmured softly, falling into the rhyming verse that they used to share. "Can I just say, I don't like seeing you this way? Why're we here? In this place of fear? This beeping beeping pierces me like a spear."

Jett felt Daddio turn away for a moment and then he was back, offering her a chair. She tried to smile, mutely ducking her head in acknowledgment as she moved it as close to Ben as she could and then lowered herself into it. Her tears fell silently.

She couldn't breathe. How could anyone hurt another person with such willful, malicious intent? Jett tried to regulate her breath, just like Ben had taught her. She choked back a sob. It took a long time before she could speak.

"I'm all out of rhymes. Will you forgive me this time?" As she spoke to Ben, Jett felt Daddio retreat to stand guard. She stared at her friend, tucking away her questions. Now was all that mattered.

But Jett was at a loss. She wondered if that happened to grown-ups, too. She didn't know where to start, what to say, or even *remotely* the right thing to do. Would she know all of that when she was an adult? At what age does one know how to handle each new situation, with all its variables? This seemed like a lot to learn. Would it just come naturally or was there a course in such things, maybe at university?

Resting her head on the bed's rails, the tubular metal seemed cold to Jett. It slowed her thinking. She realized Ben probably needed a distraction, a way out of his "now." She knew she did. Jett thought he might need a story. That's what she would want, if something trapped her in this sterile space. She would try to sleep through it, too. Who wouldn't? Ben needed a new story to replace his cold, bleak reality.

Head filling with possibilities, Jett looked around. She took a deep breath and decided to tell him of her adventures, and of love, and of all that she had learned since they were last together. Ben would hear it and love it. She knew it. He *had* to. This version of now needed some life, some fun–an adventure? *Something* to erase the isolation.

Jett looked around again. Where was Yoda when Ben really needed him?

Tears welled again, but she blinked them back. "Once upon a time, in the quiet of Tiburon, on a quaint cul-de-sac, there lived a Jedi knight in hiding…"

In a corner of the room, with no one the wiser, the hot-shot lawyer wept. He witnessed Jett baring her beautiful, unbroken soul to an unresponsive Ben. Joe Harper held his breath and prayed silently. He watched over them both. Ben would be okay. Jett needed him to be. They all did.

27

THE WEEK FOLLOWING the big win, time passed in a blur. There were trips to visit Ben, monitoring his minimal progress and endless waiting for *any* improvement—it was a lot to process. And now, unbelievably, today was the last day of school.

Exhausted, relieved, and maybe even a *little* bit happy for the summer break, Jett kept her head down as she walked toward class. One more day. The Core5 had made it through another school year. They'd won the Sophomore Sound-Off.

In the quad, Jett hoisted her backpack and bent down to run her fingers along the sweet-smelling lawn. Dew drops tickled her touch. She smiled. Like Yoda's sun-kissed fur, the blades of grass were warm to the touch and, for the very first time, she wasn't scared by the imminent arrival of another summer break. Unscheduled hours might actually be a good thing right now. Ben had a long road to recovery and, as often as he'd allow, she wanted to be there. He'd need her.

Was *this* love?

In the middle of the field, Jett stood up. She turned around to see Ruby holding Sam in a headlock and froze. Both girls were smiling, maybe even laughing. What the—? This didn't make sense on any level.

Parting from his friends headed toward the Campus Café, Andy walked over to Jett. He looked at her as if he knew what she was thinking and wanted to reassure her. "It's okay," he said, gently picking up her hand. "Ruby told us she's been taking fighting lessons and Sam must've asked to see some moves."

Jett felt tension melt away from her shoulders as she muttered under her breath. "Ah well, if Sam only knew." She turned her full attention to Andy. Would he think her stupid if she were honest with him? "I think one day we'll find out that Ruby's scary look killed someone."

Andy laughed, squeezing her hand firmly. Jett smiled up at him. When did he get so tall and how did he always know just what she needed?

Ruby abruptly released Sam from the headlock and rounded on them. "So, is this a thing?"

Jett cocked her head, confused. "Is what a thing?" She had forgotten how random Ruby's questions could be.

Andy gazed quietly at Jett for a moment before refocusing on Ruby. With another gentle squeeze of her hand, he cleared his throat.

Watching the color rise up his neck and along his jawline, Jett decided that, too, looked different.

"I hope so," admitted Andy.

Ruby seemed satisfied about something. "Okay," she said, as if she was giving her permission for something. "I mean, I can *kind of* see how this works." Her eyes ping-ponged between Andy's face and their conjoined hands as a slow grin took up residence on her face. "But didn't see that one coming. Did *you*, Sam?"

Sam shook her head adamantly. "Nope. No. Nuh-uh. I wasn't even here for most of it." But she, too, was grinning broadly. "Ruby, can you show me how to flip Andy onto the ground?"

Ruby lit up. "Sure thing!"

As both of them advanced on him, Andy dropped Jett's hand and backed up, making a time-out T with the fingers of one hand bouncing against the palm of the other.

"Um, no. Shouldn't you ask *me—you know, your victim Andy*—if that's okay? I never agreed to…"

Jett observed the exchange studiously. She wondered if this was what being friends looked like.

Both Sam and Ruby burst into laughter.

Andy dropped his hands. He wore a slow-growing smile, but that smile vanished as soon as Ruby started coming at him again. He sprinted away like his life depended on it.

Jett watched his sudden decision with interest. Maybe he *was* running for his life. It was a good defense, too. That's what they taught the girls in gym class.

With a start, she realized that something—someone—was missing. "Hey," she called out, drawing both Andy and Ruby back toward her. "Where's Carlos?"

The frolicking trio immediately turned serious, peering around the quad. Jett rolled her eyes. Sheesh! As if she hadn't already scouted the area.

Sam shrugged, puzzling to herself. "I don't know," she admitted. "I thought he'd be here by now."

"He's not usually last," Andy said, glancing down at his phone. "That would irk him. Aaaand—nope. No text. Did he let any of you know he'd be late? I'd ping him, but he hasn't responded to my last text yet."

Ruby pulled out her phone. "No text yet, but he never ignores *me*." She started tapping away.

Just in case the Princess was sidetracked by her fan club or more messages from her assistant or something, Jett sent a text, too. It wasn't like him to not show up, especially not like him to be missing and fail to tell anyone. You would think he'd know how worried they were. Where *was* he?

Ruby looked down at her phone, shook her head, and spoke at the group in her Princess command tone. "While we're waiting on our soccer star, let's address the elephant in the room."

Jett looked around. First, they were outside, not in a proper room. But an elephant? That would be exciting! Would she really get to see an elephant around here? She craned her neck, looking. Nope. No elephant in sight. She frowned.

Ruby rolled her eyes. "Jett? Jett!" She started snapping her fingers. "Stay with me here. Focus. Yes. Like that. Eyes on me." Satisfied that she'd put a stop to Jett's mind-wandering, Ruby continued in her bossiest voice. "Alrighty then! Sam? I had tutors who worked with the school the whole time I was away, but I bet you didn't. In fact, I *know* you didn't. I heard you have to take tests at the end of the summer to confirm you can be a junior. Is that true?"

Sam met Ruby's eyes as she gave a quick nod before ducking her head and examining the ground in front of her.

Ruby cocked her head, considering something. "Yeah. I thought so." Then she paused for a long time, glanced at her phone, and abruptly pinned Andy and Jett to their spots with laser focus while they endured uncomfortable silence.

At least, that's how it felt to Jett. As she stood frozen in place, she wondered if this was a precursor to the death stare and shook her head to clear such thoughts. That wasn't real. Death stares only happen in comics and movies—right? Jett remained immobile, just in case.

Hands on hips, Ruby finally got to the point. "So, you brainiacs, how *exactly* are we going to get her caught up? How are we going to save Sam and keep our Core5?"

Jett let out a sigh of relief. She knew they should wait for Carlos to figure out the summer schedule, but at least Ruby hadn't killed anyone—yet.

She ventured to speak. "Shouldn't we wait for Carlos?" she asked. "It's not like him to stand us up and then to not respond to texts. Anyone else a little worried?"

Sam dusted invisible dirt off the palms of her hands. "Nope. Not a little worried. I'm a *lot* worried," she said. "He's always come through for us. Where is he now and why isn't he answering?"

"Maybe he can't text," Andy mused. "I'll call."

He dialed and put his phone on speaker, holding it out so everyone could hear. He hung up when Carlos' voicemail came on.

"Guys, this ain't right," Sam said anxiously. "I think we need to find him. Let's go."

They all started walking.

Whispering, Jett looked to Andy and Ruby. "How does she know where to go?"

No one said anything, confirming her suspicions. Sam *didn't* know, but neither did they, and they had to do something.

"I'll call Daddio," Jett volunteered. "He'll come get us."

Just then, they heard a horn honking. Beep. Beep. Honk, honk, honk. To Jett, it sounded like a code of some sort.

Suddenly, Ruby started running, which meant her handlers were running, too. Then Sam took off, followed quickly by Andy, who easily sprinted past them all.

Jett wondered why they were running toward the lime green SUV with oversized wheels and bumpers. After it pulled into the lot and rolled to a stop, she saw Carlos hop out of the driver's seat.

"Surprise!" he yelled, grinning from ear to ear.

Andy socked him in the arm. And so did Sam, only harder. Then she threw her arms around his neck. Reflexively, his arms went around Sam, who was crying.

"You jerk. You big turd. You scared us!"

Ruby stood back and demanded. "Why didn't you answer your texts or calls?"

Carlos patted Sam on the back a few more times and disengaged. "Why, safety, of course! Safety *first, remember!* I didn't have time to connect my phone to my brand new ride. This is a *regalo* for my sixteenth birthday. No more BART for me! My Papá and Mama insisted. They said I needed my own way to get us places. Do you like it? What do you think?"

With all the tension gone, the Core5 crowded around his super-loaded-but-super-safe-SUV and cheered. Sam dubbed it "the boy toy," but Carlos called it his "Core5 Cruiser."

Tired of no longer being the center of attention, Ruby elbowed her way to the front of the group. "We need to know your summer plans, Carlos. It's time to make a schedule so Sam here can get caught up. I want her to ace all of the exams before our junior year. Are you up for it? Can you help?"

Carlos nodded. "Whatever you need, Linda."

Hands back on hips, Ruby rounded on the group. "Everyone else in?"

Jett and Andy nodded mutely.

Sam swiped at some tears and smiled.

"Okay, then! I think everyone's on board."

Andy raised his hand. Ruby's brows shot up, but he waved her off. "No, don't worry. I'm here for the summer, too. Especially to help Sam. I just—" He let out a deep sigh as he looked at his Core5. "I just—I had to make a deal to be here. You know we're usually gone as a whole family each summer, so I had to negotiate."

Ruby looked bored. She started rolling her wrist. "So—out with it."

"I kinda agreed that I would start using my real name instead of the Americanized version." He hesitated, but Jett nodded encouragement at him. "My family and community call me Anand. It means 'joy.' And since I really kind of *am* that, especially thanks to our group, I figured I would. I mean, I *can*. I will. Are you all okay with that, calling me Anand?"

Sam let out a whoop and Carlos came in for a high five. Ruby practiced saying it under her breath before she nodded. Jett was the only one not surprised. She was so glad Andy decided to be called Anand and especially happy about his reason why. After all, she was happier around her Core5, too.

A text interrupted Jett's train of thought. It was from an unknown number. Huh. That had never happened before. Reading it, she almost dropped her phone. Jett looked up at her friends and smiled in a daze. "Guys. Listen to *this*."

> Dear Jett Harper,
>
> We are happy to inform you that some of our current prospects have passed their initial training and consistently demonstrate potential for service dog work. We have selected these elite pups as possible matches for a few of our clients. They are ready to begin training specifically for the needs of their future partner. We believe you will be one of them. Would you like to meet the dogs to see? If so, we will need to set up an appointment for you and a parent or legal guardian.
>
> We're looking forward to meeting you and working together as you become part of a service dog team.
>
> Sincerely,
> Everything Pawsable

Jett looked up into the smiling faces of her Core5. Some seemed confused and hesitant, but all seemed excited. Grinning too, she started to rock and bounce on the balls of her feet.

Suddenly, her summer was very full. Jett had planned to spend time with Ben and help Sam, but now this! She shook her head in wonder. Soon, Jett would meet her very own Yoda-Gus, *her* service dog prospect.

What more could happen?

AUTHOR'S NOTE

YAY! You're here!
You've completed Sophomore Year at Presidio Prep.
What do you think? Want more?
Are you ready for Junior Year?
Then join Jett Harper and the rest of the Core5
in *Testing Time*.

To ensure your enrollment,
go to emmegrange.com & sign up.
It won't be the same without you!

xx

Emme Grange for the Core5

P.S. Why not bring others along?
Leaving a review
helps people know if we're a fit.
You make the difference.

ACKNOWLEDGEMENTS

I hardly know where to begin. So many people have made this book possible, from the technical team to the emotional support. If I listed everyone, this section would be longer than the book. Please know you are valued, named here or not.

That being true, I must give a special thanks to my Mom, my first Superfan, who is *not* a Kathy. :-) I am grateful to Kylie Sek of Cover Culture for conscious cover design and redesign. Stephanie Anderson of Alt 19 Creative used her mastery for interior layout & design. Daniel Willcocks' community of Activated Authors keep me connected. Janet Rae-Dupree poured over every line. My Soul Squad is integral to my success. They are my Core5.

And of course, there's YOU, the reader. Your time is the most valuable gift you can give to anyone, especially an author. Thank you for sharing yours with me. I write to connect and your reviews and feedback tell me if I have. *You* are why I write.

ABOUT THE AUTHOR

Emme Grange lives on stories of hope, on tales that tell us *we can*. She believes we don't have to change to be good enough. We already are, just by being ourselves.

Having spent years failing to find the missing manual, "How to Be Normal", she is *still* seeking safety, testing time and hacking hope. Emme knows what it's like to be a reluctant rebel and a peculiar person. She writes for anybody who needs a story of acceptance and everyone needing a story of encouragement.

CPSIA information can be obtained
at www.ICGtesting.com
Printed in the USA
LVHW040049250523
747942LV00003B/543